On the Ice in Antarctica

"... the stark Polar lands grip the hearts of the men who have lived on them in a manner that can hardly be understood by the people who have never got outside the pale of civilization."

ERNEST SHACKLETON, 1907

With an Introduction by Lloyd G. Blanchard
National Science Foundation

On the Ice in Antarctica

Theodore K. Mason

Illustrated with photographs, charts, and maps

DODD, MEAD & COMPANY ● NEW YORK

ACKNOWLEDGEMENTS

The author is grateful to the National Science Foundation, the
United States Navy, and the Scott Polar Research Institute for
their cooperation in the compiling of information and photographs, and
to Wallace E. Caldwell for assistance with illustrations.

Library of Congress Cataloging in Publication Data

Mason, Theodore K.
On the ice in Antarctica.

SUMMARY: A volunteer for the Navy's Operation "Deep
Freeze" provides an account of present-day Antarctica
including information about the exploration of the
continent and its geology, ecology, and role in
scientific research.
1. Antarctic regions—Juvenile literature.
[1. Antarctic regions] I. Title.
G863.M37   919.8′9   77-16856
ISBN 0-396-07535-5

*For my family, especially my mother whose
dream of travel was infectious*

Contents

Introduction by Lloyd G. Blanchard   9
National Science Foundation

1. The Worst Place in the World   11
   Volunteering   11
   The Flight South   14
   McMurdo Arrival   20

2. On the Ice   27
   McMurdo Station   27
   Food, Glorious Food!   30
   Communications   33
   Isolation Stress   35
   Personnel Selection   38
   Coping   40
   Hazards Away from Camp   44
   At the Pole   49
   Siple Station   53
   Palmer Station   53

3. Discovery and Exploration   56
   The Unknown Land   56
   First Sightings   58
   Ross Finds McMurdo   61
   The Whalers   63
   Scott's First Attempt   66
   Shackleton's Saga   70
   Race for the Pole   75
   Two Veterans Return   82
   The Air Age   86
   More Expeditions   90

World War II   91
The IGY   93
The Antarctic Treaty   96
Since the IGY   96

4. Unlocking the Frozen Secrets   98
The Ice Sheet   98
Giant Icebergs   101
Drilling the Ice Cap   103
The Climate   106
Atmospheric Studies   110
Rocks   114
Fossils   115
Dry Valleys   119
The Sea   121

5. Life in a Lifeless Land   123
Plants   123
Insects   124
Flying Birds   125
Penguins   127
Seals   136
Whales   142
Fish   143

6. Natural Resources   146
Harvesting Sea Life   146
Minerals   150
Cold Storage   152
Tourism   154
Protecting the Environment   155

Index   158

Introduction

Antarctica. Few places on earth have so completely captivated the imagination, the talents, and the energies of the young and hearty. The brief history of this great continent's exploration—barely spanning two-hundred years—is rich in the exploits of brave people who dared to go South, to be among the first, to find out what is there and what it means to the rest of us now and in the future.

The very existence of this seventh and coldest, highest, driest continent on earth was only suspected two centuries ago. Its discovery and exploration since, and the year-round scientific investigations going on there today in peaceful international cooperation among a dozen nations, represent one of the truly great achievements of mankind.

Because of its character, so remote and hostile to human life, the Antarctic has been and probably always will remain the domain of young people: despite all of the applications of modern technology by Americans and others in Antarctica today, as described in this book, it is still true that human survival in the Antarctic can sometimes depend on sheer stamina. But of far greater importance than individual human survival in the Antarctic is the survival of Antarctica, itself, as a virtually unexploited region divorced from mankind's ever expanding list of material needs at the lower latitudes. This survival will depend on the ways that tomorrow's young scientists, conservationists, and others justify the preservation of this beautiful, vast area for peaceful endeavor. My hope is that some young readers of this book will take up this cause and join the next generation of Antarcticans.

18 October 1977
Washington, D.C.

Lloyd G. Blanchard
National Science Foundation

ANTARCTICA

INDIAN OCEAN

ATLANTIC OCEAN

SOUTH ORKNEY
ISLANDS

Bellingshausen (USSR)
Capitán Arturo Prat (Chile)
DECEPTION ISLAND
Argentine Islands (UK)
Palmer (USA)
ANTARCTIC
PENINSULA

BELLINGSHAUSEN
SEA

AMUNDSEN SEA

WEDDELL SEA

General Belgrano
(Argentina)

Halley Bay (UK)

Druzhnaya (USSR)

RONNE
ICE
SHELF

PENSACOLA
MOUNTAINS

Siple (USA)

ELLSWORTH
LAND

MARIE BYRD LAND

Sanae (RSA)

Novolazarevskaya
(USSR)

QUEEN MAUD LAND

Syowa (Japan)
Molodezhnaya (USSR)

Mawson (Australia)

Davis (Australia)

Amundsen-Scott
South Pole (USA)

Vostok (USSR)

Mirny (USSR)

Casey (Australia)

WILKES LAND

Dumont d'Urville (France)

Leningradskaya (USSR)

VICTORIA LAND

DRY VALLEYS

TRANSANTARCTIC
MOUNTAINS

Scott Base (NZ)
McMurdo (USA)

ROSS ICE SHELF

ROSS ISLAND

ROSS SEA

90° E

180°

90° W

0

STATUTE MILES

0   100   200   400

200

South
America

Africa

Antarctica

Australia

New
Zealand

1. The Worst Place in the World

VOLUNTEERING

The middle-aged, balding yeoman sauntered into the Armed Forces television control room at the Guantanamo Naval Base, Cuba. His grin was devilish.

"What's wrong with you?" I asked, annoyed at the interruption.

He laughed mysteriously. "How do you like ice?"

"Ice?" I scrutinized him, wondering what he could be talking about. But, delighting in the suspense, he refused to elaborate. Instead he said, "They want to see you up at Personnel."

The rest of the television crew looked curiously at each other. "What for?"

"And you think *this* hole is the worst place in the world!" the yeoman smirked as he marched out of the soundproof room.

Suspecting a joke, I drove to my barracks and changed into tropical dress whites. I walked nervously under the tall palm trees to the small, clapboard building at the edge of Bay Hill and waited for the personnel officer to emerge from his office.

"Your request has been approved," he said. I suddenly realized what had happened. At my previous duty station, I had volunteered for Operation "Deep Freeze," the Navy's Antarctic task force that provides support for the National Science Foundation's Antarctic Research Program. I hadn't been accepted because that season the support program had plenty of journalists. Now, a year later, someone at the Bureau of Naval Personnel had remembered my application, even though I had forgotten about it.

"You don't have to accept the orders," the lieutenant said hopefully. He was worried about finding my replacement rather than my future of cold toes.

Welcoming the opportunity to escape the isolation and boredom of Guantanamo Bay, I opted for Antarctica, even though I knew little about it except that it sounded like a chance for adventure. Whatever, it certainly would be a change.

I suffered several weeks of jokes about penguins and Eskimos before flying to the United States for a period of indoctrination, during which I learned there were penguins near the South Pole, but no natives. (The Eskimos live at the opposite end of the globe, I was told.)

After being judged physically and mentally fit, I joined the airlift of men and supplies traveling 8400 nautical miles from the East Coast via California, Hawaii, and Pago Pago to Christchurch, New Zealand, where the Navy maintains the advance headquarters for the United States Antarctic Program.

The operating season usually begins in early October and continues through February, which is the spring-fall period in the Southern Hemisphere. At this time of year in Antarctica, temperatures are at their warmest and the sun shines twenty-four hours a day, permitting work around the clock, if necessary.

Each season, the Navy's Antarctic Development Squadron SIX (VXE-6) makes over one hundred flights between Christchurch and McMurdo Station on Ross Island, off the antarctic coast. The 2400-mile trip south is particularly hazardous because the planes have nowhere to make an emergency landing except in the freezing South Pacific.

VXE-6, which proudly calls itself the world's only antarctic airline, uses seven LC-130 Hercules to carry passengers, scientific equipment, important supplies, and mail to the United States stations. The personnel of other countries working in Antarctica aren't as fortunate. Usually, they must wait for news from home and fresh provisions until their resupply ships can make it

Ski-equipped LC-130 Hercules takes off from antarctic coast.   U.S. NAVY

through the ice during the summer. Other countries, particularly Argentina, Chile, and the United Kingdom, also fly in Antarctica, but not as extensively as the United States.

The VXE-6 "Hercs" are specially adapted for cold-weather work. Skis, coated with Teflon to keep them from sticking to the ice, are fitted around the wheels of the Hercs and can be lowered over the wheels for landings on packed snow or ice. The planes are also equipped with special navigational devices, lubricants, and high octane fuel for extreme cold-weather operation.

Between October and December, Air Force C-141 Starlifters are used to supplement the Hercs of VXE-6 in the airlift to the "Ice." Later, two Coast Guard icebreakers, a cargo ship, and a fuel tanker arrive at Port Lyttleton near Christchurch. After refueling and taking on fresh provisions, the ships will eventually form a convoy heading for McMurdo Station.

In the spirit of international cooperation that characterizes work in Antarctica, the United States also provides transportation to the Ice for New Zealand scientists and their equipment. The United States, in return, is allowed to use facilities near the Christchurch airport as a staging base and an advance headquarters that is staffed year round.

The United States also assists the Royal New Zealand Air Force with flight information during the height of the summer when New Zealand Hercs join Deep Freeze in support of New Zealand's Scott Base, located near McMurdo on Ross Island.

During the summer season, about three thousand men from thirty countries invade Antarctica. The United States program, as run by the National Science Foundation, sends over three hundred scientists and one thousand support personnel, mostly Navymen and civilian technicians hired by a California contracting firm, Holmes & Narver. The National Science Foundation spends $7,500,000 in grants for 130 research projects and another $37,500,000 for logistical support, maintenance of stations, and use of ships.

THE FLIGHT SOUTH

At the advance headquarters, special cold-weather clothing is issued to wear on the Ice. The Navymen wear heavy, green cotton uniforms, while the scientists and civilians don more colorful garb, usually plaid shirts, wool trousers, and the bright red parkas that make a person easier to spot in "the field," the white, desolate landscape of Antarctica.

Everyone of course wears heavy underwear, thick socks, and the unique thermo boots. Looking like footwear for astronauts, these boots are constructed to trap air between two layers of rubber. The air insulates so effectively that feet stay warm in the coldest temperatures with only one pair of socks.

Typical antarctic clothing consists of three layers: long underwear, heavy cotton or wool trousers and shirt, plus outer trousers and green or red parka with fur-trimmed hood. The outer trousers, called "mini-pockets" because of their numerous pockets, and the parka have heavy wool liners that can be buttoned inside for protection against very cold weather. Both outer garments are treated to make them wind-resistant.

Getting dressed is difficult, but once ready, the newcomers report to the airport and join the strange mixture of men and women headed "South." You can tell who are civilians and who are the military men by their dress. The passengers talk in small

Two Navymen, dressed in cold-weather clothing, visit Scott's Hut near McMurdo Station.   T. MASON

groups, but every one appears careful to conceal his increasing excitement.

If the weather permits, numerous flights are launched daily from Christchurch to deliver personnel to relieve the crews that "wintered-over" on the Ice. The "Old Antarctic Explorers," OAE's, they're traditionally called, have withstood six months of continual darkness, bitter winds, snowstorms, and temperatures from $-60°$ to $-100°$ Fahrenheit. With their beards, pale skin, and red eyes, they look like mountain men or cavemen emerging from some dark wilderness as they leave the plane. They tend to stare at grass and trees and traffic as though recalling cherished memories.

Solar storms on the surface of the sun may keep the planes from flying to Antarctica because the radiation they produce interferes with long-distance radio communications. On other occasions, strong head winds en route or snowstorms at McMurdo may force a plane to return to Christchurch. When a plane reaches the "point of safe return" during each flight, approximately halfway, the pilot must decide if the weather conditions and the fuel supply favor a safe arrival at Williams Field at McMurdo. It's a difficult decision to make because the weather can change before the plane reaches the airfield.

A startling example occurred one October when six planes took off in succession from Christchurch to open up McMurdo Station after the winter. Five of the planes reached Williams Field safely, but a blizzard blew up just before the last plane was due to arrive. The storm was so severe that emergency crews waiting in tracked vehicles at the edge of the ice runway couldn't see the plane.

The pilot circled until all of the fuel was used. Then, relying on radar readings, he tried to set the plane down. He almost made it, but the landing gear collapsed. The plane skidded, tearing off one wing. While the eighty men aboard began making their way out of the plane, one of the burly sailors was so anxious he jumped out

Broken pieces of sea ice cover the ocean along the Ross Ice Shelf.

T. MASON

of his seat, with the seat belt still fastened, tearing it from its fittings.

Some of the men, like dazed penguins, wandered away from the plane, and it took several anxious hours to rescue them because of the storm. All at Christchurch waited through the night for the radio message that no one was seriously injured.

Most of the eight-hour flight south usually is a boring, uncomfortable ride inside the cargo hold of the Herc. Except for a few porthole windows, forward and aft, the cargo area is a windowless tunnel that vibrates enough to scramble your brains. Conversation is difficult because earplugs are worn by many in a feeble attempt to muffle the noise. Most people settle back into the strap seats and try to read or take a nap. A few study the instructions on how to operate the elaborate camera equipment they bought at the duty-free shop in Christchurch.

The VXE-6 flights aren't equipped with smiling attendants, but you can help yourself to coffee or water when you want it. Once you pass the point of safe return, the cargomaster hands out "C" rations. Each small carton contains a choice of tuna fish or ham, crackers, fruit salad, and brown pudding. The meal seems a fitting introduction to the tough life you expect lies ahead.

During the trip, the pilot usually invites a few of the passengers at a time to visit the flight deck to look out of windows that wrap around the nose of the Herc. Unfortunately you can see little except sky, a few passing clouds, and the dark-blue Pacific 35,000 feet below. But then, as you near the continent, the first white specks appear floating on the ocean.

"Icebergs," the pilot points out.

Because of the distance, the icebergs seem to be tiny, but many are huge. They are formed when the tips of glaciers pouring down from the high interior of the continent break off at the coast.

Lovely, geometric patterns of ice begin to form on the ocean until it eventually becomes a solid, frozen sheet. Your excitement builds. Suddenly, the sharp, white mountains of Victoria Land pierce the horizon, heralding the antarctic coast. In the cargo

*Huge glaciers cut through the Victoria Land Mountains from the high
interior of the continent to the sea.* T. MASON

hold the passengers scramble to try to see out one of the port-holes.

When the Herc reaches the mountains, the pilot turns left and heads the plane along them toward McMurdo Sound. Now the view is spectacular. Cut by huge rivers of ice, these mountains form part of the Transantarctic Mountain Range, one of the longest in the world, which divides the western and eastern regions of Antarctica. Although the ice covering gives the appearance of a single continent, western Antarctica and the Antarctic Peninsula are actually groups of islands connected by ice to the mainland area, the eastern area.

The sun is usually shining in the summer, making the white landscape blinding to look at without sunglasses. As well as the mountains, the Ross Sea below is covered with thick ice. It's difficult to believe that the Coast Guard icebreakers will be able to smash through it in early January when they begin breaking open a shipping lane to McMurdo Station.

Icebreakers actually don't cut through ice. The reinforced bow rides up on the ice and the weight of the ship breaks it. Still, the icebreakers often get trapped in heavy ice or become stranded when ice damages the propellers.

To help overcome these problems, two new icebreakers have

United States Coast Guard icebreakers open a sea lane to McMurdo Station. Mount Erebus is in the background.   U.S. NAVY

been put into service by the Coast Guard. The *Polar Star* and the *Polar Sea*, commissioned in January, 1976, and January, 1977, respectively, were the first to be built by the United States since 1954 when the 310-foot *Glacier* was launched. More powerful than the Glacier class, ships of the Polar series are 399 feet long and can cut through twenty-one feet of ice.

Flying above the route the icebreakers will take, the Herc continues along the coast until Ross Island appears from the air as a large, snow-covered mound in the plain of ice. Rising twelve thousand feet from the center of the island, a white volcano puffs clouds of smoke into the brightest, bluest sky you can imagine.

"Mount Erebus," the pilot announces to those delaying as long as possible their departure from the flight deck.

Many stories have been fabricated about this strange volcano. Some say it marks the entrance to a world inside the earth. One author has written that unidentified flying objects come from inside Mount Erebus.

Scientists, however, have found only that the lake of lava inside the volcano is expanding and approximately two small explosions occur each day.

As the plane begins dropping in stages, the pilot tells the passengers to buckle up. He also warns that he is lowering the cabin temperature to match that on the ground at Williams Field. The temperature, he announces, is only —10° Fahrenheit. Those who expected Antarctica to be colder, at least for their arrival, look disappointed. Many places in United States are as cold as ten degrees below zero in the winter. The difference is that it's summer in Antarctica.

McMurdo Arrival

As the Herc passes Mount Erebus, McMurdo Station appears strung out on the slopes of Ross Island, facing the great Transantarctic Mountains across the frozen strait of McMurdo Sound. At first sight, the station looks like a frontier town that wasn't designed but merely grew up there on the windy, ice-blanketed slopes of the island.

McMurdo Station, however, was planned, or rather its location was. The site was picked in 1955 because it is one of the few places in Antarctica that is free of ice and snow during the short summer. Scientists estimate that only 4 per cent of Antarctica is not covered by ice.

McMurdo is also important because it is the closest point from the sea to the South Pole, one of the most scientifically important locations on the continent. It costs less to fly men and supplies from a staging base at McMurdo to the South Pole than from any other point along the coast.

The advantage of McMurdo's location was discovered by Captain Robert Scott of the British Royal Navy. His expedition built a hut there in 1902 and made the first attempt to penetrate the interior of the continent. But later explorers used this hut far more than its builders did.

As the Herc skirts Ross Island, New Zealand's Scott Base appears on the opposite slope. Weddell seals can be seen basking in the sun, and huskies leaping against their lines are staked into the ice nearby. New Zealand, Australia, and the United Kingdom are the only countries that continue to use dog teams for transportation in Antarctica, in addition to motor sledges and tracked vehicles. Dogs have been found to be often more reliable than

In early October, McMurdo Station lies blanketed in snow from the antarctic winter. Scott's hut is in the foreground. T. MASON

machines in the cold climate. Dogs don't break down, and they're good companions during long periods of isolation on the Ice. As a result, dogs still have a place in antarctic logistics.

Both Scott and McMurdo stations are located in the Ross Dependency, a sector claimed as New Zealand territory. The question of who owns the territory, however, has been put aside temporarily through the agreement of the Antarctic Treaty.

Beyond Scott Base lies Williams Field which was built in 1956. Holmes & Narver is presently rebuilding the camp, which is now half-buried in the Ross Ice Shelf, an extraordinary barrier of ice as large as Texas. Permanently attached to the continent, the ice shelf ranges from six hundred to fourteen hundred feet in thickness. Large tabular icebergs continually break off the seaward edge, while the ice shelf moves north at about four feet each day as the result of pressure from the glaciers feeding into it.

As the plane continues its descent, the passengers sit silently waiting, listening to the whine of the turbo-prop jet engines. The heavy skis are lowered into place under the wheels, further slowing the Herc. Then with a sudden rush and a thud, the transport touches down on a snow-compacted skiway, made by Navy personnel using special machines. The Herc bounces gently as the pilot taxis it to the parking area near the bright-orange control tower.

Everyone jumps up before the plane stops and begins to wrestle his sea bag of heavier clothes and his camera from under his seat. The door opens, admitting a blast of what's to come, bright light and cold air. In anticipation, the passengers adjust their sunglasses as they crowd toward the small opening. Then one by one they step precariously down the short ladder to the unknown.

Taking your first step in Antarctica can seem as exciting as arriving on the moon. You recognize that there is no place like this on earth. Immediately, the cold invigorates you. Your nose and lungs tingle with the clean, frigid air. Your eyes water and your nose runs in the 10-mph wind, which makes the temperature feel as though it were —31° Fahrenheit. Under such conditions, you could contract frostbite in a few minutes. Frostbite is the freezing of exposed flesh and can become serious if allowed to

Williams Field huts are half-buried in winter snow on the Ross Ice Shelf. U.S. NAVY

continue. The frozen area dies from lack of blood circulation and turns black. Usually, everyone protects himself against frostbite or else stays indoors. But when you first arrive in Antarctica, you're not so confident. In your thoughts is the reminder that you're in the coldest region on earth.

The incredible white landscape, completely barren and yet so beautiful under the clear sky, compels you to stop and gawk. On the left, the majestic Transantarctic Mountains mark the actual coastline. In front of you, the canvas and wood huts of Williams Field appear half-sunk in the hard-packed snow. Two reassuring flags stand out among the three short rows of huts—the American and the Red Cross of the medical dispensary. Beyond, you can see Ross Island, blinding white and imposing beneath the smoking

23

Mount Erebus. In such a setting, anything is possible, even UFOs.

Feeling a little tipsy with excitement, you take a deep breath of the cold, rarefied air and begin to hurry as fast as your thermo boots will allow across the frozen snow after the other passengers. As you walk, you continue to gaze at the white landscape and marvel that the air is so clear you feel you can see forever.

In front of a dilapidated hut that has experienced many storms, you join your fellow travelers in boarding an orange shuttle bus with abnormally large wheels. Once everyone is seated, the bearded, tough-looking driver slams the bus into gear and spins off as though pushing for the lead position in the Indianapolis 500.

After less than a mile, the Ross Ice Shelf ends and the driver is forced to slow down at the point where the shelf meets the frozen sea ice and becomes McMurdo Sound. Cautiously, the bus wiggles its way down a small embankment onto the frozen ocean.

In January the icebreakers will cut up a large part of the Sound, and, with the help of the wind and ocean currents, push the ice out to sea, leaving open water around McMurdo Station. The ice shelf, a few miles away, will remain attached to the base of the coastal mountains.

Before the ice is chopped up each year, the road to McMurdo Station becomes potholed as a result of the sun's melting the ice and seals' gnawing through breathing holes. The shuttle bus bounces when it hits these holes or sinks momentarily into them. For some this is a thrill, but the danger is very real. For example, Seabee Richard Williams died when his tractor went through the ice during the construction of the airfield, which has been named for him.

When the road over the ice to McMurdo becomes completely unusable, the Navy builds a new snow road along the edge of the ice shelf to Scott Base for use during the remainder of the summer.

Each arrival in Antarctica is somewhat different. On this first trip, the sun was beaming brightly although a cloud bank loomed in the distance on the seaward side of Ross Island. Because of our

A tracked vehicle heads toward coastal mountains across frozen Mc-Murdo Sound. T. MASON

excitement, no one paid any attention to the clouds. But as we zoomed along the six-mile road to McMurdo Station, the sun quickly disappeared. Suddenly the bus was surrounded by a bright, dense fog, and strong winds began to buffet us from side to side.

The driver stopped the bus and radioed command headquarters at McMurdo: "Shuttle One. Mac Center."

"I read you, Shuttle One," a voice answered.

"Shut down one mile from base. Waiting out storm." The burly constructionman's voice was matter-of-fact. Being an OAE, he had been through many storms before, or at least that was what he wanted us to believe.

"Roger, Shuttle One," the voice from headquarters replied. "Mac Center out."

The driver lit a cigarette while the rest of us sat anxiously staring at the white wall pressing against the bus windows. We didn't realize that we were experiencing a "whiteout," the storm condition most feared on the Ice. During a whiteout, it's impos-

sible to tell direction. Everything looks the same: bright white. Pilots caught in such a storm say they couldn't even tell whether they were flying the plane right-side up.

Smoking meditatively, the bearded Navyman took off his sunglasses and surveyed us. He abruptly asked two men sitting nearby if they were "Airdales," the nickname for Navy aviators.

"Yep," One of the VXE-6 crew answered proudly. "Puckered Pete's Blue Ribbon Boys. That's us."

The driver snorted contemptuously. He coughed and screwed up his face as though something stank on the bus. I was to find that the keen rivalry among the different military units, as well as between the military and the civilians, was usually good-natured. But it could deteriorate as quickly as the weather because of the close living conditions and the stress of being in such a harsh environment.

The whiteout fortunately lifted as rapidly as it had set in. There before us stood McMurdo Station, dazzling in a fresh frosting of snow. You could hear everyone on the bus sigh with relief.

"Okay, folks! On with the show!" the driver called out as he started the engine.

2. On the Ice

McMurdo Station

Because of its location, McMurdo is the largest and busiest station in Antarctica. The installation serves as operation center for most United States activities on the Ice. Nearly all personnel and supplies arrive either by ship or plane at McMurdo. (Staff and cargo for Palmer Station on the Antarctic Peninsula are resupplied via Argentina.)

From McMurdo, VXE-6 airlifts the designated personnel and equipment to inland stations and field camps. In addition to the Hercs, the squadron uses UH-1N "Huey" helicopters, based at McMurdo, to support the many field parties conducting research in the area.

McMurdo's population swells to about eight hundred during the summer, with seventy remaining for the winter to maintain the station and conduct some experiments. Of the wintering-over complement for 1977–78, all were Navymen except six scientists and two contractors from Holmes & Narver. Unlike the other stations, which are run by Holmes & Narver, McMurdo is operated by the Navy for the National Science Foundation. In the early years of Deep Freeze, the Navy was responsible for all of the stations.

McMurdo has everything you would expect to see in a small

Main street, McMurdo Station, where the winter darkness lasts for 4½ months U.S. NAVY

town: living quarters, offices, warehouses, chapel, movie theater, store, barber shop, library, pool hall, laundry, post office, fire house, and hospital. All of these are small facilities, however, and the buildings that house them are not like those of a typical small town. Connected by a scramble of electric lines, pipes, and paths, they are a strange mixture of grim huts and sterile, two-story structures that look like warehouses.

Despite their uninviting appearance, the new warehouse-like buildings have improved life at McMurdo by replacing many of the dilapidated huts, originally built as temporary quarters and offices. The new structures, although they have few windows, have plumbing, central heating, and more space than the old huts.

One of the new buildings, a complex that looks like an aircraft hangar, has enough rooms to house the entire wintering-over crew. It also has the station's dining halls, only store, barber shop, laundry, pool hall, and library. Because most of the important facilities are located in this one building, the men don't have to venture outdoors in bad weather.

The new dining halls are divided into one area for enlisted men and another for officers and civilians. This unfortunate division tends to emphasize the segregation of these groups. The former mess hut served as a morale booster when everyone, including the commanding officer, waited in the same line and all ate together. At the other stations, which are much smaller than McMurdo, a sense of esprit de corps is enhanced because everyone dines together.

McMurdo also boasts a modern sewage and water system, which no other station has. Sea water is pumped from under the ice of McMurdo Sound and distilled by evaporator units into 12,055 gallons of fresh water daily. Carefully wrapped pipes, mounted above the frozen ground, deliver the fresh water to those buildings blessed with plumbing. The pipes are protected by a special heat tape to prevent freezing.

In the older quarters, one man is assigned each day to hand-carry water for drinking and washing. Called the "house mouse," he also airs out the hut and cleans it. A similar system of sharing the chores at other stations includes taking turns cooking when the outpost is too small to have its own cook.

Because the ground around McMurdo is permanently frozen, the station is plagued with the problem of sewage disposal. Raw sewage is piped into the Sound beside the shoreline of Ross Island. Emptied fuel drums used to collect urine and plastic sacks of solid refuse are hauled to the shore and later floated out to sea

McMurdo Station boasts largest building in Antarctica.   U.S. NAVY

on ice floes after the icebreakers open the summer sea lane. The National Science Foundation maintains that the sewer from Mc-Murdo Station is nothing compared to what the Weddell seal colonies in the area excrete into the Sound every day.

An incinerator was planned to be built at McMurdo to burn the station's trash, but the project proved to be uneconomical because of the amount of fuel needed for its operation. The Navy, as a result, ships some inorganic matter back to the United States on the empty supply ship each summer. Organic and some inorganic material is floated out to sea, but this is nothing compared to the amount of garbage and abandoned equipment dumped into the Sound during the early years of Deep Freeze.

Another important change in the operation of McMurdo was the removal of the station's nuclear power plant. The first to be located in a remote area, the nuclear power installation had provided the base with desalinated water from the Sound and with electricity for a decade. It took from 1973 to 1976 for the plant to be dismantled and the nuclear wastes and contaminated soil and rock shipped back to the United States for disposal. Such care was necessary because the Antarctic Treaty prohibits the dumping of nuclear waste material, however slightly contaminated, in Antarctica.

Fresh water and electricity, now produced by diesel-powered generators, are carefully conserved because of the cost of shipping the fuel from the United States. Showering is limited to a quick soap and rinse once a week. Consequently, a shower becomes a special occasion. But the cost of providing fresh water is not the only reason behind this limitation of showers. Too much washing dries out the skin, which becomes easily chapped in the cold, dry antarctic climate.

At other stations, snow must be shoveled into snow-melters to produce water. The pertroleum used to power the melters has to be flown from McMurdo, adding to the transportation cost of the fuel.

FOOD, GLORIOUS FOOD!

Because of the lack of recreation and variety, eating plays an important role in making life on the Ice more tolerable. The

Men unload supplies from the first plane in after the winter. At least some of the eagerly awaited fresh provisions will reach the isolated stations of the interior. U.S. NAVY

major stations have full-time cooks who strive to serve attractive meals despite the lack of fresh vegetables and dairy products. They make up for the missing perishables by serving a variety of canned and frozen items. On occasion, fresh vegetables and fruits are flown in on one of the Hercs from New Zealand, and some of this produce manages to reach the men at inland stations before being gobbled up.

Favorite main dishes include steak with mushrooms, lobster tails, and shrimp Newburg, which come from frozen supplies. The cooks do some baking of breads and desserts, too. Soft ice cream is the most popular of the desserts, which is proven by the grumbling whenever the machine breaks down. Chopped nuts and a variety of toppings are available to satisfy anyone's sweet craving.

Cooking on the Ice often demands a special skill and a great deal of patience. Because of the extremely dry climate, cinnamon rolls baked early in the morning at McMurdo become hard by the end of breakfast. Add undercooked powdered eggs to this menu and your day is ruined!

At the South Pole Station, low air pressure because of the high

Navy cooks help to counter the effects of isolation by preparing excellent meals. U.S. NAVY

altitude (over 9000 feet above sea level) increases a cook's challenge. One man's first attempt at a meringue pie exploded after thirty seconds. At that altitude, normal amounts of baking powder make food jump right out of the pan because the gas expands so quickly. Other ingredients must be adjusted as well, forcing the cooks at the inland outpost to develop their own recipes.

Many people gain weight on the Ice as a result of overeating and drinking out of boredom, even though their bodies require more calories for energy and warmth in the cold climate. These people don't get enough exercise to burn up the excess calories because either machines do most of their work or their jobs may not require strenuous effort. Sometimes it is too cold to do any work or even walk outdoors. Other people, however, may lose weight despite eating three or four meals a day because they work hard and burn up lots of energy in the low temperatures.

Overeating is a dramatic indication of how much the antarctic cuisine has improved since the days of the early explorers, who had to calculate carefully their daily ounces of biscuits, dried meat, tea, and cocoa. These men had a filling meal when they caught a seal or penguin or were forced to kill one of the dogs.

COMMUNICATIONS

Although men on the Ice today eat better than their predecessors, their isolation is much the same. No newspapers or radio and television stations link Antarctica with the rest of the world. McMurdo does have a one-page news sheet called *The Sometimes.* Handed out at the breakfast table each morning, it summarizes the world news received by radio messages. The newspaper was given its name because it appears spasmodically. The reasons vary, from poor radio reception to the editor's not getting out of bed in time.

McMurdo also boasts a small radio station, AFAN, which broadcasts mostly taped music in the station area. Some "live" programs are created by the journalists and other enthusiasts for the men to listen to after work.

A United States post office is maintained at McMurdo as well as other stations serviced by the air squadron during the summer. The mail service, however, varies according to the weather and the number of flights from Christchurch. Usually it arrives once or twice a week. Letters are usually weeks old when received and the cookies Mom baked with love are stale and crumbled. But the men are glad to get them, nonetheless.

Those who collect stamps and canceled envelopes have special interest in the antarctic postal system. From all over the world,

In the mess hall of a remote field camp, men enjoy the ample meals prepared for them. U.S. NAVY

philatelists send letters and postcards for the postal clerks to cancel and stamp with the seal or emblem of the units working at the particular station where the post office is located.

By using a special radio-telephone patch system, personnel stationed on the Ice can call home at times, which helps to make up for the erratic mail service. The radio calls are relayed by amateur radio operators, "hams," in various parts of the world to the caller's hometown telephone operator, who connects the radio transmission to a telephone call. The procedure is often difficult because of the differences in time zones and in the hours when ham operators are on the air, talking to each other around the world.

It is usually worth the effort, but the opposite effect can occur if the person you are calling isn't at home. Such a failure can make men on the Ice depressed for days because they mistakenly believe nobody at home cares about them.

In addition to telephone calls home, radio communications are crucial to all stations and operations on the Ice. Often these communications may be interrupted by solar flares and other disturbances in the ionosphere. The interruptions may last for days or weeks, during which time the crews and scientists working in Antarctica have no information about the rest of the world.

Such disturbances in radio communications happen because of an interaction between the ionosphere and particles given off by the sun during solar flares. About fifty miles above the earth, the ionosphere is filled with tiny electrically-charged particles, somewhat like metal objects, that can reflect radio waves. Because radio waves don't travel very far in a straight line, the ionosphere can be used as a reflector to bounce the radio waves from one point to another point on the globe. Communications satellites are used in a similar way to broadcast programs to other countries.

But the ionosphere loses its reflecting ability when particles carrying an electrical charge shoot in from outer space and collide with its charged particles. Antarctica is more vulnerable to this problem than other land areas because the lines of force from the earth's magnetic field curve inward at the magnetic poles, drawing the charged particles in that direction.

34

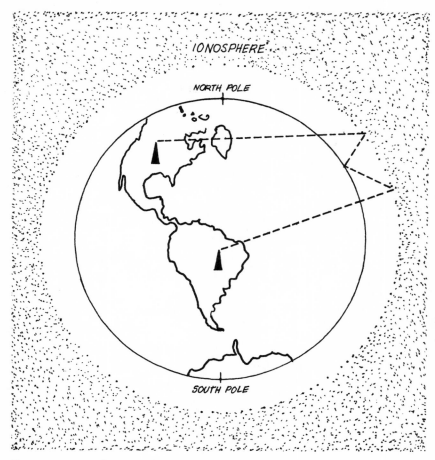

Long-range radio communication is possible by bouncing the radio waves off the ionosphere. W. CALDWELL

ISOLATION STRESS

Simple activities such as showering, eating, drinking, receiving a letter, or making a ham patch to the folks back home take on greater significance on the Ice because they help to break up the monotony of the daily routine and the lack of variety and stimulation in the environment. They also provide relaxation for the men who work long hours, seven days a week, with only half a day off on Sunday to attend religious services. Everyone seems to be in a race against the sun, which circles around the sky but never sets during the period from October to March. Scientists must take

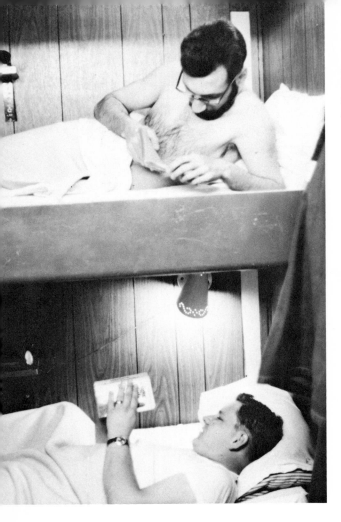

A good book at bunk time helps to provide some escape from the lonely polar winter at McMurdo Station.

T. MASON

advantage of the good weather in order to finish their research before darkness and the fierce cold set in.

When you first arrive on the Ice, it is sometimes difficult to sleep because there is no change from day to night. This affliction, if you should catch it, is called "the big eye." It's a way of saying you can't sleep, even though you feel exhausted and your sleeping quarters are totally dark. In your mind you know the sun is still shining outdoors. During the winter darkness, the situation is reversed, but the problem remains the same: the big eye.

The hostile physical environment, however, is not the most difficult aspect of living on the Ice. According to scientific studies, the worst problem is in adjusting to the enforced intimacy of a closed, isolated group of people for a long period.

Difficulty adjusting becomes more evident during the winter when there are fewer "new faces" around and less activity. The depression begins as other men begin leaving for home. For many, the most depressing part of the long winter comes when the last Herc departs, dipping its wings in farewell as it passes overhead. At McMurdo, the final plane leaves about February 22, the cut-off date because the period of darkness is quickly increasing each day.

Work begins on sealing the buildings to keep out the increased blowing snow. Cracks are taped and then stapled. Tin cans are used to cap stove chimneys and exhaust pipes. The outdoor lighting is checked thoroughly. Roads and trails are marked with red and green flags tied on six-foot bamboo poles.

The night lengthens to fourteen hours and the sun at noon is barely visible on the horizon. At McMurdo the final sunset glows above the distant hills on April 24, although a period of twilight will continue for about a month. All hands are assembled facing the sun for a solemn ceremony. The Flag is lowered and presented to the outstanding sailor of the year.

As the sea freezes for a hundred miles around the continent, the men begin to realize that their isolation is almost complete. Only on a few occasions has VXE-6 made emergency flights during the winter to rescue seriously injured men, one of whom was a Soviet

As the winter clamps down on McMurdo, the men have a lot of digging out to look forward to in the spring. U.S. NAVY

exchange scientist working at Byrd Station. At such times, fuel drums are set on fire to light a landing area for the two Hercs, flying together in case one runs into trouble. Nothing else can be done to aid the operation. Sudden storms and mechanical problems that could develop en route are the risks accepted by the rescue crews.

The symptoms of isolation on the Ice begin to show up as alteration of sleeping patterns, depression, irritability, loss of enthusiasm, staring states, poor concentration, and memory gaps. Physiological as well as psychological factors may play a part in these behavior problems, such as vitamin B-1 deficiency due to high consumption of alcohol. However, sufficient research has not yet been done.

A man who may appear normal during the summer can change into a different personality as the winter progresses. He may lack self-discipline, dwell on minor problems, fail to get along with others, and start drinking heavily. He also becomes a bit paranoid and believes no one really cares about or understands his problems. Personal habits of others can be intolerable, even the way someone eats, talks, or laughs. The weaknesses or mistakes of others also become unbearable, and the unfortunate individual is blamed and hated for them.

Among the most serious behavioral problems encountered were a civilian who turned from a pleasant to a dangerous companion when winter came and another who walked out into the darkness and was never found.

PERSONNEL SELECTION

Those who cope best with the isolation and close living conditions have certain traits in common. To begin with, they are sociable, but not overbearing. The life-of-the-party type soon gets on everybody's nerves. Those who do the best on the Ice are also versatile and can be satisfied doing whatever job they are given. At times, they also need the ability to withdraw into themselves to escape the others, especially during the winter when it's impossible to get away from them for any length of time. At McMurdo one year, the photographer withdrew to the photo lab, emerging

Two pilots join a Halloween party at McMurdo Station. T. MASON

only when he ran out of food and when commanded to muster at all-hands meetings. He earned the nickname "Phantom of the Ice."

Those best suited for life on the Ice enjoy such unsophisticated things as food, movies, trivial conversation, cards, darts, and model ships. They must be able to distinguish important from unimportant issues, but most of all they must have a sense of humor. Practical jokes are often played. For instance, on the Fourth of July, the New Zealanders from Scott Base like to attack McMurdo and force their captives to drink tea in retribution for the destruction of Crown property by the Americans' forefathers at the Boston Tea Party. The appearance of ghosts and the tracks of big-footed monsters are almost annual events. Santa Claus has appeared at the South Pole, apparently having lost his sense of direction. Wintering-over crews particularly enjoy frightening newcomers with such stunts as displaying wild men locked in cages.

All who are to spend long stretches on the Ice are supposedly screened by medical and psychiatric tests. However, the psychiatric examinations, based on an attitude questionnaire and one-hour interview, are not particularly effective. Candidates are queried about their attitudes toward their parents, their sexual and drinking habits, and why they want to go to the Ice. The

written questions encourage many to lie if they want to be selected for antarctic duty. I know I did, and others have admitted to it, too.

In addition to the inept testing, some Navymen with questionable personality traits are allowed to go South because they are needed in a particular job. In the early days of Deep Freeze there was an excess of volunteers among the military support personnel; today some have to be drafted from other Navy assignments. Civilian contractors and scientists and their students reveal fewer adjustment problems as a rule, probably because they are more submerged in their work, which is usually more rewarding than maintenance and other routine jobs in the operation of a station.

Perhaps the most important factor in the selection of personnel is similarity of interests and habits—for example, men living together should get along well if they are either all neat or all slobs.

Coping

To prevent behavioral problems, station authorities strive to keep everyone busy at work and occupied during off-duty hours.

One of the VXE-6 Herc pilots strings Christmas decorations on an internal fuel tank during a long photo-mapping mission over the continent. T. MASON

Part of this strategy to create a normal pattern of living is the insistence that everyone keep to a schedule as much as possible.

For recreation, the station leaders often appear willing to do

This Navyman used his leisure time at McMurdo Station to build a hot rod from spare parts. T. MASON

LEFT: *Drill holes + dyna-mite = fishing, antarctic style.* U.S. NAVY

BELOW: *Ice football, any-one?* U.S. NAVY

anything to create diversion, as long as it's indoors. On special occasions, such as birthdays and the traditional holidays, they stage celebrations that may include costume contests, dart tournaments, and a carnival night to raise money for charity.

The cooks contribute by preparing birthday cakes or special meals which assure the events of importance and success. On St. Patrick's Day, the cooks turn everything on the menu green, from the pineapple rings on the baked ham to the dehydrated mashed potatoes. Somehow they also manage to find appropriate decorations for the dining halls.

Another device is to create new antarctic holidays to bolster interest in the passing of the time, particularly during the winter. These holidays include the day of the annual sunset, mid-winter's day, the day of the annual sunrise, and the day of the redeployment home. On these occasions, the men are usually given a half day off from their jobs and many groups celebrate by throwing parties.

One winter, the station commander decided to create additional days to celebrate by compressing the calendar so that Thanksgiving, Christmas, New Year's Day, and other holidays occurred again during the months of March through September.

With all the ice and mountainous terrain nearby, McMurdo should be ideal for winter sports, but station authorities haven't encouraged them because of the risk of accident. Injuries are difficult to treat properly, even though McMurdo has a doctor and a well-equipped medical dispensary. Moreover, a person with a serious injury has to be airlifted to New Zealand and a replacement found to do his job, which costs money and could delay projects from being finished by the end of the summer.

Because of the close confinement at McMurdo, someone—maybe you—may feel the need to get away from the others for a while. Where to go then becomes the problem. You can climb up Observation Hill, separating McMurdo from Scott Base, and survey the spectacular view of the Transantarctic Mountains in front of you, the ice shelf on your left, and the back of Ross Island to your right.

You can also ask for the key to Scott's hut at Hut Point, on the other side of the station, and add your name to the log of visitors who have marveled over the historic site and the state of the provisions left behind on the shelves. The unopened canned goods look almost new because the cold, dry climate has preserved them. The only change is the addition of overhead beams to guard against the collapse of the roof from heavy snow.

Outside the hut under the veranda, designed like the outback buildings on Australian properties, you can still see some of the fodder for the ponies that Scott brought on his second expedition.

So much for the sight-seeing.

HAZARDS AWAY FROM CAMP

Because of the lack of things to do at McMurdo, you may feel the urge to take a stroll away from the station. But going off alone anywhere on the Ice can be dangerous, even fatal. A blizzard could blow up without warning and trap you. Or you could fall

Crevasses on the slopes of Ross Island await the unwary. T. MASON

A "Weasel" tracked vehicle, with trailer, heads over an ice ridge.

into a crevasse, a deep crack in the ice which is often concealed by a thin layer or "bridge" of snow. You can sink to your waist in the chasm or fall hundreds of feet into it.

Because of the hazards, no one is allowed to leave the station without permission. Even then, you have to carry a survival sea bag of heavy clothing and take a friend along. In case something happens to you, your buddy supposedly can return to the station for help.

Not everyone, of course, obeys the rules all the time. One Christmas Day, after services in the Chapel of the Snows, four of us malcontents decided to go skiing. Taking the VXE-6 Weasel, a small tracked vehicle, and skis from the rescue equipment, we drove around the edge of Ross Island toward the ski slopes marked off by the New Zealanders from Scott Base. On the way we took turns being pulled by the Weasel across the ice shelf, and we shed our shirts in warm sunshine to pose quickly for "Antarctic Hero" pictures.

When we reached the slopes, halfway around Ross Island, we skied for awhile, then decided to head back before we were missed. But the Weasel stalled unexpectedly after riding over a small ridge of ice, and the driver impatiently ran down the battery trying to start it again. Cursing, he looked under his seat and

45

*Author, left, and companion pose quickly for "Hero of the Antarctic"
picture during memorable skiing trip on Christmas Day.* G. LITTLE

discovered that the spare battery had been removed! Suddenly,
we were stranded. We had no radio and no one knew where we
were.

We argued about who was at fault and what to do. Finally, we
decided that the two best skiers would return to McMurdo for
another battery while the driver and I waited with the vehicle.
Having only the two pairs of skis, there really was no other
choice.

The driver and I watched silently as the two figures slowly
disappeared as though swallowed up by the blinding light radiat-
ing off the ice shelf. The two of us joked and talked intermittently
until a heavy bank of clouds appeared over the ski slope behind
us. The sun quickly disappeared and the temperature dropped
dramatically. We put on the heavy outer layers of clothing from
our sea bags and stared anxiously into the grayness as the sky
became overcast.

Before long, the driver decided we would keep warmer if we
built an igloo by cutting blocks of ice out of the ice shelf. He
grabbed a shovel and tried laboriously to force it into the ice.

Two men examine tracked vehicle stalled on the ice. U.S. NAVY

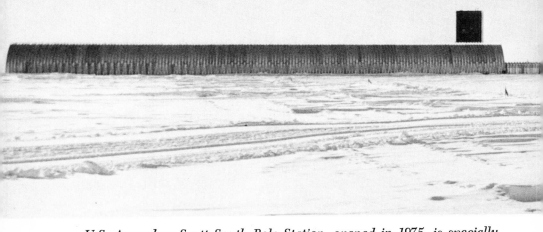

U.S. Amundsen-Scott South Pole Station, opened in 1975, is specially

Giving up, he returned angrily to the Weasel, and we continued a now silent vigil.

Although we didn't dare talk about it, we both knew our companions might get lost or fall into a crevasse. We waited, haunted by the knowledge that we could do nothing to keep from freezing to death if our friends didn't return in time. We couldn't walk to McMurdo because of the danger of getting lost in a storm, and we had no way to signal anyone.

Feeling hungry as well as cold, we opened the "C" rations we fortunately had thrown in our sea bags before leaving McMurdo. We savored what we knew might be our last meal, then continued watching in silence for our companions. It seemed that we couldn't think of anything to talk about that would help keep us from dwelling on our predicament. Although it was too cold to sleep, I closed my eyes and struggled to imagine fireplaces, summertime, and other memories of being warm.

"Hey!" the driver suddenly shouted. "There they are!"

As I bolted up and squinted into the grayness, the driver flung open his door and started racing across the ice. I thought he had gone crazy. Then in the distance I saw the two figures skiing toward us, and I started after the driver. As we ran waving our arms and shouting, I could see that they were pulling something behind them on a sled.

48

designed to avoid snow and ice accumulation.   U.S. NAVY

They seemed embarrassed when we greeted them with Russian bear hugs.

"What took you so long?" the driver demanded.

They looked at each other, then grinned at us sheepishly. "We stopped at the chow hall."

We stared at them in disbelief. How could they have thought of their stomachs when we were freezing to death? Of course, they were wise to get something to eat when they had the chance, but we didn't appreciate that at the time.

"Come on, let's get this battery in the Weasel and get out of here," one said, starting toward the vehicle.

With the battery installed, we crept back to McMurdo. The Christmas party was over in our hut when we entered. There were only a few men in the lounge who inquired how our party had been at Scott Base.

"Unbelievable," we told them as we dragged past to our bunks.

Afterward, we four had a reverence for station regulations.

AT THE POLE

About 850 miles south from McMurdo, Amundsen-Scott South Pole Station is situated on the polar plateau of the interior, 9,200 feet above sea level. It is named for the first two men to reach there.

Most people refer to the South Geographic Pole simply as the "Pole." It is the end of the earth's axis of rotation, marking the southernmost point of the earth.

The first station at the Pole was built during 1956–57 for the International Geophysical Year. However, it became covered by drifts, the weight of the snow crushing it slowly into the ice cap until the buildings couldn't be used any longer, even with heavy timbers to shore up the ceilings. Once buried, the station was also caught up in the movement of the ice, like a log in a stream.

The site for the present station was chosen at a point one-quarter of a mile away from the exact location of the Pole so that five years after it was built the station would have drifted over the Pole. After several years of testing the effects of drifting snow on a small scale model, the new station was opened in 1975, at a cost of six million dollars.

Designed to save it from the fate of its predecessor, the present station is distinguished by an aluminum geodesic dome sixty feet high which protects three two-story buildings inside. The dome-shaped design, plus the rounded design of the connecting structures, allows snow to blow over the station without collecting on top of it in any heavy amount.

The dome is unheated, making the temperature inside about zero degrees Fahrenheit. It also has a hole in the top to let accumulated heat escape. No matter how well insulated, any building loses heat, which melts the snow blown around it. The resulting moisture causes the building to deteriorate. This moisture also creates ice when it refreezes, forming a heavy weight that eventually can crush the building.

Inside, the outpost is probably the most luxurious of any on the Ice. It has wood paneling, wall-to-wall carpeting, an observation deck, and a lounge with a large tinted plate glass window and skylights so scientists can observe auroras during the winter darkness.

In addition to the main station, a small emergency camp has been set up a short distance away to store half of the station's supplies. In case of fire, the men would have emergency food and equipment. The flags of all the Antarctic Treaty Nations, formed in a circle, are also located near the main station.

A crew of approximately thirty civilians during the summer and twenty in the winter work at the station, which is ideal for special atmospheric research because it is isolated from the pollution and noise of the world. The station is also the receiving site for reports from two satellites in polar orbits around the earth, as well as part of the worldwide network that monitors earthquakes.

For anyone who goes to the Ice, the South Pole is the ultimate experience, the top of the mountain. Few, however, have a chance to visit it because of the limited space available on the VXE-6 summer supply flights. Other than those assigned to work there, usually only newspaper reporters and distinguished visitors invited by the National Science Foundation have the privilege. But they can miss out if the weather is too cold, such as −60° Fahrenheit. Despite their alterations for extreme cold weather, the Hercs might be damaged while waiting on the ground. Extreme cold temperatures can freeze the hydraulic system in the planes, cause breaks in the rubber around electrical systems, or crack the engine metal. Even in less severe temperatures, the pilot keeps the turbo-props turning for fear that he might not be able to start the engines if they were shut down for any length of time.

Preparing to land at the Pole, the pilot warns each passenger to steer clear of the turning props when leaving the plane and to walk slowly because breathing would be difficult. The oxygen in the air is less than at lower altitudes, and during the short air trip from McMurdo passengers haven't had time to become adjusted to the altitude. Men stationed there usually take several weeks to acclimatize, although some have more trouble than others, with such difficulties as not sleeping, headaches, and nosebleeds.

The pilot also warns visitors about the extreme cold which, despite the brilliant sunlight during the summer months, is never above zero degrees. Usually you can expect the temperature to be about −25° Fahrenheit, with a light wind blowing to make it feel much colder.

Regardless of the warnings, someone among the visitors inevitably becomes overexcited and has to be given oxygen to restore normal breathing. Or someone stays too long outside the station taking pictures and suffers a frostbitten nose or fingers.

Frostbite sets in quickly at the South Pole, for workers and visitors alike.

T. MASON

For instance, one year we had great difficulty in convincing a news reporter that his nose was turning white and he had better go inside the station where he could warm up. The reporter had to be forced inside, but at least it saved his nose from serious frostbite.

In addition to the station and the flags, there is only a vast plain of frozen snow to see, but its starkness and brilliance are awesome. If you're lucky, you might even get to see the air glitter, much the way in which a snowscape glitters in the sun. One of the research projects at the station is trying to determine the source of the rain of ice crystals responsible for the effect. Called clear air precipitation, this phenomenon produces a considerable part of the ice accumulation on the polar plateau. It falls almost constantly during the winter night and from 50 to 75 per cent of the time in the constant daylight of summer. A laser probe, aimed directly upward, is being used to trace the origin of the crystals.

Life at the South Pole for the men stationed there is similar to that of other small outposts where it is crucial that all get along well together. Living conditions are even more cramped than at McMurdo which, by comparison, seems like a small town. The men at the South Pole are also isolated for longer periods than those at McMurdo because the colder weather restricts the number of months during which air operations are possible. Studies of the effects of isolation on the men are therefore an important part of the scientific research conducted at the station.

Men at the Pole have to endure special problems because of the extreme dryness and high altitude. Injuries take longer to heal and simple surgery becomes a major operation. Even the cooks have problems. Because water boils at a higher temperature than at lower altitudes, it takes longer to prepare food. And they have to watch out for those exploding pies!

SIPLE STATION

Like the first outpost at the South Pole, Siple Station at the base of the Peninsula lies buried under drifted snow now. Construction of a replacement facility nearby began during 1977–78. Usually, ten employees of Holmes & Narver operate the station during the summer and five remain for the winter.

Siple was first opened on a limited basis in 1971 when Byrd Station in Marie Byrd Land was being phased out as a year-round facility. Thirteen miles of radio antenna that had been stretched over the snow were moved to Siple so that upper-atmospheric-physics research could continue.

The outpost is appropriately named for Dr. Paul Siple, who made his first trip to the Ice as a Boy Scout with Richard Byrd's first expedition. Although he was only nineteen, Siple did the work of a man, according to Byrd. On a subsequent Byrd expedition, Siple served as the scientific leader. He also became the first scientific leader of Amundsen-Scott South Pole Station, in 1956.

PALMER STATION

Palmer Station on Anvers Island adjacent to the Antarctic Peninsula is an important port for oceanographic ships, especially the *Hero* operated by the National Science Foundation.

Towers at Siple Station lead to a 13-mile dipole antenna used for upper atmosphere physics research. U.S. NAVY

Shore of Antarctic Peninsula near Palmer Station   u.s. navy

Because the facility is easily accessible by sea from South America, tourist ships such as the Lindblad *Explorer* can also reach the station.

Palmer is important as a place to study weather, ice, plants, and animals. It is one of the locations on the continent where plants (in the form of flowering grasses) can grow because of the warmer climate. Men on the Ice refer to this area as the "banana belt." The temperature here averages 26° Fahrenheit, and about 23 inches of precipitation fall each year, making the Peninsula atypical of the rest of Antarctica.

The station is run by twenty civilians during the summer and seven in the winter.

3. Discovery and Exploration

THE UNKNOWN LAND

People believed in the existence of a south polar continent long before anyone saw it. Ancient Greek scholars thought Antarctica was needed to balance the land areas of the north. They called it "Antarktikos," meaning "Opposite the Bear," referring to the northern constellation they could see in the night sky. The early Polynesians also had legends about the existence of a white land in the Pacific to the south. Historians believe their canoes may have been stopped by the ice when they were exploring.

European mapmakers at the time America was discovered imagined a great continent in the waters south of Africa. They called it "Terra Australis Incognita," the "Unknown Land." Many voyages were made to try to find this fabled continent, which was believed to be populated and laden with riches. Explorers discovered islands around Antarctica which they believed were part of the great southern continent. They not only claimed the islands for their countries but also all land lying further south.

Captain James Cook of the British Royal Navy was the first to get an accurate idea of what Antarctica was really like. Cook, who explored the coasts of Australia, New Zealand, and other South Pacific islands, sailed completely around Antarctica between 1772 and 1775. His ship, the *Resolution*, probed the ice

Scott's cross at McMurdo marks the gateway to the continent once known as the Unknown Land. T. MASON

pack on several sides of the continent. The closest approach was within one hundred miles of the continent, near the point where Japan's Syowa base is located today. Because of the great expanse of the ice pack and the giant icebergs, Cook believed an ice-covered land and not the fabled land of legend was situated farther south.

Although he never sighted this continent, Cook reported fur seals on South Georgia Island and the South Sandwich Islands in the South Atlantic, 150 miles northwest of what is now called Queen Maud Land. The news brought money-hungry American and British seal hunters to the subantarctic islands because coats of seal fur were in great demand at the time.

First Sightings

These sealers were probably the first actually to see the Antarctic continent rather than the ice around it. We can't be sure because they didn't keep accurate records and jealously guarded their discoveries of seal colonies from competitors. One of these sealers, Nathaniel Palmer of the United States, sailed the west coast of the Antarctic Peninsula in November, 1820, searching for seals. On his sightings, the United States bases its claim to discovery of the continent. But some historians, after looking over the log books of other sealers at the time, believe his discovery claim is questionable. It's likely that Palmer saw nothing more than offshore islands.

Earlier that year, in January, two other men reported seeing the continent. The British explorer Edward Bransfield was cruising along the rugged shores of the South Shetland Islands when bad weather forced him to turn southward. He reported seeing land near the area of Hughes Bay on the western side of the Peninsula. But whether he saw offshore islands or land, no one can be sure. He, like many others, could have been confused because the frozen sea and ice-blanketed islands near the shore of the continent often appear to be one piece of frozen land.

At the same time as Bransfield's sighting, the Russian explorer Thaddeus Bellingshausen was discussing with his crew their sighting of land a little farther south at the base of the Peninsula.

The area he named after Czar Alexander I of Russia turned out to be extensive islands near the coast.

Today's historians tend to agree that none of these three men should be credited with discovering the continent, even though they probably sighted it. They did no more to prove its existence than Captain Cook had when he sailed around it fifty years earlier.

In 1821, Bellingshausen accidently met Palmer near Deception Island off the Peninsula coast in one of the most colorful episodes of antarctic history. Even in this event, no one can agree on exactly what happened.

According to the romanticized American version, Palmer's ship was trapped in fog when he heard voices close at hand. The fog cleared to reveal two Russian warships, one on either side of him. The Russians invited him aboard the *Vostok*, where he told Bellingshausen he had discovered a vast tract of land to the south. Bellingshausen profusely complimented the young American and offered him lunch.

But according to Bellingshausen's account of the meeting, the

59

visibility was good all day. "At ten o'clock we entered the strait and encountered a small American sealing vessel," the Russian wrote matter-of-factly in his ship's log, as though such meetings occurred every day in unexplored antarctic waters. Palmer described sealing activities in the area to him but didn't mention any discovery of land. Russian scholars also say that Palmer wasn't served lunch.

Unless new documents come to light, the question of discovery is likely never to be answered satisfactorily, nor will we know for sure if Palmer got any lunch.

Also disputed is the claim by the United States of the first known landing on the continent, when Captain John Davis sent a boatload of his sealers ashore at Hughes Bay on February 7, 1821.

One sealer who contributed to antarctic exploration about this time was the Scotsman James Weddell. From 1822 to 1824 he explored the sea, notorious because of its impenetrable ice covering, between Queen Maud Land and the Antarctic Peninsula.

In 1823, Weddell penetrated the ice to a point within two hundred miles of the coast, where the British station Halley Bay is located today. Even modern icebreakers have failed to make it farther south through the ice of what is now called the Weddell Sea. James Weddell also brought back the first species of the inshore seal which was named for him.

James Biscoe, a British sealer-explorer, discovered Enderby Land in 1831 and named Cape Ann, the first name applied to a feature of the main continental mass, the eastern region of Antarctica.

If a scientific yardstick is applied, the honor of discovering Antarctica probably should go to Lieutenant Charles Wilkes of the United States Navy. During 1840, he led an expedition of four unsuitable and ill-equipped ships along 1500 miles of the coastline south of Australia. Although some of his sightings of land at various points have been questioned, Wilkes established for the first time that Antarctica was continental in size and not a large piece of floating ice.

Wilkes is described as cantankerous but brave and resolute. He took on the trouble-plagued expedition after four other officers

Lieutenant Charles Wilkes, LEFT, *United States Navy* U.S. NAVY. *Sir James Clarke Ross,* RIGHT, *Royal Navy* NATIONAL PORTRAIT GALLERY, LONDON

had resigned or flatly refused to accept the leadership. Only his iron will can account for the achievements that were gained.

Ross Finds McMurdo

In addition to discovering a large portion of Antarctica that today bears his name, Wilkes contributed to further antarctic discovery by describing his voyages in the letters and maps he sent to Captain James Ross of the British Navy. Captain Ross, however, was angry at Wilkes, as well as at the French navigator Dumont d'Urville, for selecting an area they supposedly knew his expedition planned to explore. In 1839, D'Urville had explored the coastline near the spot where France now maintains its scientific station. D'Urville named the coast and the penguins he found there after his wife, Adélie. Considering the comical nature of the Adélie penguins, some people have wondered if his wife really felt honored.

Instead of following in the "footsteps of the expedition of any other nation," Ross decided to sail south from Tasmania and steer a more easterly course than Wilkes and D'Urville had. Ross didn't know that the British sealing captain John Balleny, in the summer of 1839, had taken this same route and reached 69° South. At any rate, Ross' decision was to have historic results.

Ross had previously spent ten years in the Arctic and, in 1831, had discovered the North Magnetic Pole. He hoped to duplicate this success by being first to reach the South Magnetic Pole.

Because of his previous Arctic experience, Ross' antarctic expedition was better prepared than those of Wilkes and D'Urville. His two ships, *Erebus* and *Terror*, were the first to be strengthened for working on ice; they had double decks, double hulls, watertight compartments, and reinforcing beams. In addition, the crews were carefully picked and well equipped.

In January, 1841, Ross boldly sailed through drifting pack ice. No one before him had dared to enter this treacherous ice, which has the power in its movement to trap ships or crush them. On a day of fog and storm he cleared the ice field and entered an open sea that was later named for him. Four days afterward, when the snowstorm and thick fog dispersed, the expedition was stunned to behold a new land of snow-covered mountains.

Sailing past the dark cliffs of Cape Adare, Ross neared the spectacular peaks and named them the Royal Society and Admiralty ranges. At Possession Island he sent a party ashore for twenty-five minutes. They collected rocks and some penguins, the first to be brought back from Antarctica.

Ross continued on and entered McMurdo Sound. There he discovered an ice-covered island and smoking volcano which he named Ross Island and Mount Erebus, respectively. His expedition witnessed the largest recorded eruption of Mount Erebus when flame and smoke shot two thousand feet into the air.

His hope of finding an unimpeded route to the South Magnetic Pole, however, was dashed as high cliffs of ice loomed up as far as he could see. These he called the Great Southern Barrier, but we refer to them today as the Ross Ice Shelf.

Ross spent the two additional summer seasons of 1842 and 1843 exploring the ice shelf and the Antarctic Peninsula. At one point his ships just missed being crushed by icebergs during a violent storm. On another occasion, while sailing through the pack ice, Ross and his crew sighted the rarest of southern seals, which was named in his honor.

Ross' exploration was the most important of the nineteenth century, because it was from the McMurdo Sound area that the first land journeys toward the South Geographic Pole were to be launched fifty years later.

THE WHALERS

From about 1843 to 1893, only occasional efforts were made to learn more about the continent, although explorers and scientists in many countries tried to overcome government and public apathy about antarctic exploration.

It was left to the whalers to revive interest in the Antarctic. Whalers became interested in the frozen continent because their traditional arctic fishing areas were nearly exhausted by the end of the nineteenth century. They were convinced whaling in the Antarctic would be economically feasible because of reported sightings of large numbers of whales. In addition, new methods of whaling had been developed, particularly steam-driven boats armed with harpoons fitted with explosive heads.

The first whaling trips, however, were commercial failures. In 1892 a Scottish venture sailed in four old-fashioned whaling ships to the Weddell Sea. Guided by Captain Ross' reports, they were equipped for slow-moving humpback, right, and sperm whales. To their dismay, they found only the faster fin whales that spouted at them and sped away. The expedition, however, was to be remembered for one of its naturalists, William Bruce, who later commanded his own expedition to the Antarctic.

The second pioneering attempt, led by the Norwegian captain Carl Larsen, was somewhat more successful. During 1892, Larsen made important discoveries along the coast of the Antarctic Peninsula on the Weddell Sea, including the large ice shelf that today bears his name.

On his return to Norway, Larsen reported his findings to Svend Foyn, who had developed the explosive harpoon. Foyn was encouraged by Larsen's report to give financial support to a private expedition led by Henrik Bull, who was eager to capitalize on Ross' sightings of plentiful whales in the Ross Sea. In a refitted whaler renamed *Antarctic*, the expedition sailed from Norway in September of 1893 to Australia. The crew did some unproductive sealing and whaling around New Zealand's Campbell Islands before the ship was overhauled in Australia and departed for Antarctica in September of 1894.

In Australia a young Norwegian teacher, Carsten Borchgrevink, asked to join them. Because Captain Leonard Kristensen wasn't allowing any passengers on his ship, Borchgrevink was signed on as an ordinary seaman. He was to become the ship's one-man scientific staff and an important figure in antarctic history.

The Bull expedition found few of the whales Ross had claimed were plentiful, but in January of 1895 four of the men gained fame when they became the first to go ashore on the main continental mass of Antarctica. (This first landing is distinguished from that of Davis in 1821 on the Antarctic Peninsula.)

Although thousands of penguins on the beach vigorously resisted them, the party managed to stay for three hours at Robertson Bay near Cape Adare. They hurriedly collected some stones, moss, seaweed, and a few penguins, then returned to their ship. Such was the first collection of scientific information from the continent itself.

In August of 1895 Borchgrevink traveled to London where, addressing the Sixth International Geographical Congress, he urged the establishment of a base near Cape Adare, from where he believed a sledging party could reach the South Magnetic Pole. The Congress adjourned with the resolution that "the exploration of the antarctic regions is the greatest piece of geographical exploration still to be undertaken" and recommended that scientific societies throughout the world work to accomplish this before the end of the century. Although there was no immediate response, a new aspect of antarctic exploration was established. Soon no expedition could hope for support, whether public or private, without a scientific program.

Borchgrevink eventually succeeded in obtaining the sponsorship of Sir George Newnes, a pioneer of modern popular journalism in England. An old Norwegian whaler was fitted with new

A modern-day team of huskies at New Zealand Scott Base. The first dogs used in Antarctica were brought by the explorer Borchgrevink in the late 19th century.   U.S. NAVY

engines, and Borchgrevink gathered together a small but able group of men, including four scientists. The ship's captain was Bernhard Jensen, who had been the second mate on the Bull expedition. Borchgrevink also took ninety Siberan dogs. Seventy-five of them were safely landed at Robertson Bay and became the first dogs used for antarctic sledging.

The expedition built two wooden huts, and Borchgrevink and nine men remained behind when the ship, the *Southern Cross*, returned to New Zealand in February of 1899. These men were the first to spend a winter on the continent. Although he subsequently made some sledge journeys and discovered insects and quartz, Borchgrevink was later criticized for his lack of initiative in doing field work. Later explorers, however, were to learn that he had been unlucky in selecting a site surrounded by sheer cliffs that virtually turned his base into a prison.

The *Southern Cross* returned and picked up the expedition in February of 1900 and sailed along the Victoria Land Coast, and to Ross Island where Borchgrevink landed briefly near Cape Crozier. The expedition also went ashore at a site on the Ross Ice Shelf which Ernest Shackleton was later to name the Bay of Whales. This four-mile-wide inlet, where the ice shelf dips to seventy feet above the sea, was to become one of the most important locations in antarctic exploration.

From Borchgrevink's experience came the procedure for later conquest of the continent. A base camp initially would be set up during the brief summer; after the winter, sledging journeys could be made during the following summer.

With Borchgrevink began what is called the "Heroic Era" of antarctic history, a time when poorly equipped adventurers faced the unknown with great courage. From their failures and successes, the techniques of antarctic exploration were learned.

In March, 1898, the Belgian explorer Adrien de Gerlache led an expedition that made new discoveries in the region of the Peninsula and sailed to a point eighty miles off the Ellsworth Land coast. His ship, the *Belgica*, became beset by ice and drifted for twelve harrowing months. Two of the party members were later to become famous explorers: Frederick Cook as a rival to Robert Peary in the conquest of the North Pole, and Roald Amundsen, who conquered the South Pole.

SCOTT'S FIRST ATTEMPT

The most famous of all the early heroic explorers was Robert Scott of the British Navy. Although he had no polar experience or even any interest in it at first, Scott impressed the president of the Royal Geographical Society and was appointed commander of the National Antarctic Expedition. Scott's first antarctic undertaking was launched in March of 1901, using a strong but uncomfortable ship, the *Discovery*.

Scott sailed from England to Port Lyttelton, where he replenished his stores and departed for the Ross Sea on December 21,

66

1901. After discovering the King Edward VII Land Peninsula, the expedition moved along the Ross Ice Shelf to the Bay of Whales.

It quickly became evident how inexperienced Scott's men were in antarctic exploration. Four men were carried off among the ice floes for five hours on a chunk of ice that suddenly separated. Then a 24-hour sledging journey over the ice shelf revealed that two of the men with arctic experience couldn't remember how to start their stove.

While at the Bay of Whales, Scott became the first man to explore Antarctica from the air when he ascended eight hundred feet above the ice shelf in a balloon. Ernest Shackleton went up on the same day, February 4, 1902, and took the first aerial photographs of the continent.

The expedition proceeded to the rocky promontory on Ross Island, soon to be called Hut Point, and built a 36-square-foot-hut for its quarters.

One of the first sledge journeys Scott sent out from Hut Point was to Cape Crozier on the opposite side of Ross Island. "Our ignorance was deplorable," Scott wrote later. Led by Charles Royds, the executive officer of the expedition, the journey revealed that the men didn't know what or how much food was required, how to use the cookers, how to put up their tents, or even how to wear their clothes properly. On the return to Hut Point, the frostbitten men were trapped by a blizzard only a few miles from the hut. As they groped their way down the hill, George Vince and one of the huskies hurtled to their doom off the cliffs now called Danger Slopes. A memorial cross which the party erected still stands at the tip of Hut Point.

A number of sledging trips were made to lay depots of food and supplies for the following year's journeys to explore the McMurdo Sound area. During one, Scott experienced his first difficulty with the dog teams. They would hardly pull the sledges, forcing Scott to build his supply depot short of his goal. On the way home, the dogs raced quite willingly, to Scott's chagrin.

During the first winter at Hut Point, Scott imposed strict Naval discipline on the party, even the civilians, who didn't appreciate the military rule. But they all got along fairly well. There were a few fights and one man was put in irons twice for insubordination.

Scott kept the men occupied preparing the equipment for the sledging parties planned to search for routes through the coastal mountains to the unknown interior. He also sent Royds and a party around to Cape Crozier to leave a message telling the relief ship where the expedition had camped and that the *Discovery* was frozen in the ice nearby.

The major southern and western sledging journeys began in November of 1902. Scott commanded the southern party, taking with him Shackleton, Edward Wilson, and the dogs. Before Scott's group had covered much distance, the dogs had trouble pulling the sledges and looked sick. The dogs were undernourished because their staple food, Norwegian stock fish, had become tainted and was thrown out when the *Discovery* crossed the tropics on the way from England.

The men soon became ravenously hungry and suffered from snow blindness and a mysterious disease now known to be scurvy. When they camped on Christmas Day, Shackleton surprised them with a small sack containing a Christmas pudding he had hidden in a spare sock before leaving Hut Point. As a finishing touch, he also produced a sprig of artificial holly to complement the festive treat.

On the last day of 1902 the group was forced to start back, after reaching 238 miles south, the farthest point any man had been up to that time. They had opened the way to the South Geographic Pole, one of the greatest geographic prizes yet to be won. Shackleton, however, coughing and spitting blood, was dangerously ill. The others were in poor health, too. One by one the dogs died or were killed in an attempt to keep the others alive.

Returning to Hut Point, the men were cheered by the expedition and the relief ship *Morning* which had arrived with fresh supplies. Shackleton, who was bitterly disappointed at being sent home by Scott, and all who wished to leave returned on the *Morning* while the *Discovery* remained frozen in the ice near the base.

The other main journey that year, by the western party, was an equally determined attempt to penetrate the Victoria Land Coast across McMurdo Sound to the west of Hut Point. Led by Lieutenant Albert Armitage, the second in command of the expedition, the group eventually sledged up the Ferrar Glacier. At an elevation of nine thousand feet, they became the first men to see the vast polar plateau of the interior. Among this party was Petty Officer Edgar Evans who later was to become one of the first men to travel the plateau to the South Geographic Pole.

The second winter at Hut Point passed more comfortably for the expedition. They had learned much from experience, including how to cook in antarctic conditions. They also knew each other better.

After the winter, two long journeys were made from Hut Point. The first, led by Scott, followed Armitage's discovery of a route to the polar plateau. Scott, Evans, and William Lashley sledged up the Ferrar Glacier and pushed across the ice cap for eight days until forced by their dwindling food supplies and physical condition to start back. While struggling through a storm to find the head of the glacier, Lashley slipped and all three went tumbling down an ice fall. Fortunately they weren't seriously injured and the sky cleared suddenly, revealing the landmarks they needed to find their way. They also fell into a crevasse before finally making it down the glacier and back to Hut Point.

The support group that had accompanied Scott part of the way in the beginning of his journey explored six hundred miles of new country. This group traveled eight thousand feet up the Taylor Glacier, where they found fossil plants in coal shale beds in exposed sandstone.

The second major journey of the summer, led by Lieutenant Michael Barne, surveyed two hundred peaks to the south of Hut Point. Reaching the first depot laid by Scott on the Ross Ice Shelf thirteen months previously, the men were puzzled to find it had moved 608 yards. Their observations provided the first definite evidence of ice shelf movement.

Professor Wilson made two trips to the emperor rookery at Cape Crozier while these two major sledging journeys were underway. He studied penguin behavior and had the opportunity to see emperor penguins leaving their rookery as Adélie penguins were arriving at theirs, five miles to the north on Ross Island. He also brought back two chicks, one of which survived for three months aboard the *Discovery*. Little had been known about penguin behavior up to this point.

As a result of its exploration and scientific observations, Scott's first expedition was the most significant to enter Antarctica to date. It opened routes that later explorers would follow to the interior of the continent, including the South Geographic Pole. Scott also inspired and trained many who were to follow him in the conquest of the "last frontier."

Other nations sent important expeditions to Antarctica during this period, including a Swedish one in 1901 that explored the east side of the Antarctic Peninsula by sledge. After leaving a wintering party on the continent, the expedition's ship became crushed in the ice of the Weddell Sea. The men of the ship's crew were forced to spend the winter on the ice living off seals and penguins until they were rescued in 1903.

A German venture, under Erich von Drygalski, in 1902–03, discovered what now is called the Wilhelm II Coast. Leaving his steamship, Von Drygalski walked fifty miles over the sea ice to inspect a volcanic cone. This explorer is also remembered for being compelled to use penguins to stoke the ship's furnace when it ran out of fuel.

Shackleton's Saga

Ernest Shackleton returned to Antarctica in 1907 at the head of his own expedition. In addition to proving himself after being shipped home by Scott, Shackleton's objectives were to explore King Edward VII Land and reach both the South Geographic Pole and the South Magnetic Pole.

As well as ponies and dogs for transportation, Shackleton brought a specially designed car, the first antarctic vehicle, which

Shackleton's antarctic automobile SCOTT POLAR RESEARCH INSTITUTE

he planned to use to pull supplies during his trek to the South Geographic Pole. Having absorbed some of Scott's distrust of dogs for sledge hauling, he put his faith in the ponies and the car. But the car became troublesome in the antarctic conditions and could only be used on short trips to help lay supply depots. It was not till fifty years later that great traverses would be made across the continent using tracked vehicles better built to withstand the cold.

With fifteen men, Shackleton set up his winter quarters at Cape Royds on Ross Island. After the winter, he led a party across the Ross Ice Shelf, killing the ponies as he went and storing the meat at depots for the return journey. The party searched the coastal mountains for a break until in December of 1908 they saw an awesome glacier which led like a road to the Pole, the route Scott had sought during his first expedition. Shackleton named the glacier, the world's largest, for Sir William Beardmore, his financial backer.

Battling cold, hunger, and treacherous surface conditions, Shackleton led his men up the glacier to within ninety-seven miles of the Pole. They suffered nosebleeds and headaches because of the altitude; then a blizzard struck and the temperature plummeted to −70° Fahrenheit. When he realized he had done the best he could, Shackleton decided to turn back, short of his goal, without risking the lives of his men. They planted the Union Jack on the polar plateau and claimed it for the British Empire. During the 117 days of the journey, Shackleton's party sledged 1600 miles.

While Shackleton was climbing the Beardmore, a second major party comprised of Professor Edgeworth David, Douglas Mawson, and Dr. Alistair Mackay departed from Cape Royds. The goal was to reach the long-sought South Magnetic Pole, as well as to make a general geological survey of the Victoria Land Coast during the 500-mile trek to the magnetic pole and back.

This group of three, called the northern party, pulled a heavily laden sledge across McMurdo Sound to Cape Bernacchi, near the Ferrar Glacier. Improvising a Union Jack out of a handkerchief, they planted the "flag" and claimed possession of Victoria Land for the British Empire on October 17.

The party sledged along the coast, struggling across rough snow surfaces, and over sea ice that often had cracks as wide as six or ten feet. Fearing the ice would break out and destroy their return route, they left farewell letters to their families at a depot established on November 1. They also realized they didn't have enough food to make the complete journey according to the time-table previously worked out. Deciding to try out Mackay's earlier experiments of using seal blubber for fuel, they constructed a stove from a biscuit tin and killed a seal. When they poured seal blood rapidly into boiling oil, they discovered a kind of "grey pancake" which they devoured.

Continuing on, the men struggled through soft, ankle-deep snow and suffered from lack of sleep, due chiefly to the use of a three-man sleeping bag in which they had to endure each other's kicking and snoring.

One amusing but near tragic incident occurred on December 9. The leader, David, decided to take a short stroll away from camp while Mawson was at work changing photographic plates inside the tent.

Out of the silence Mawson became aware of a gentle voice calling him.

"Hallo!" he answered.

"Oh, you're in the bag [tent] changing plates, are you?" Mawson heard David say.

"Yes, professor," Mawson responded.

There was silence for some time. Then Mawson heard David calling in a louder voice, "Mawson. Mawson!"

When Mawson answered, David replied, "Oh, still changing plates, are you?"

"Yes," Mawson said.

More silence followed. Then in a loud and anxious tone, David called out again.

"What is it? What can I do?" Mawson demanded.

"Well, Mawson," David said apologetically. "I am in a danger-

It was from the edge of a crevasse such as this that David dangled while politely waiting for Mawson to finish his work and come to his rescue. U.S. NAVY

ous position. I am really hanging on by my fingers to the edge of a crevasse, and I don't think I can hold on much longer. I shall have to trouble you to come out and assist me."

Such self-effacement and extreme courtesy characterized not only David but also many of the daring early explorers, especially those who were British or of British descent. (David and Mawson were both Australians.) Without these men, there might not have been any "heroic period" of antarctic history.

The northern party eventually reached the South Magnetic Pole on January 16, 1909, and took possession of the area for the British Empire.

RACE FOR THE POLE

Shackleton's achievements clinched Scott's determination to return to the Antarctic and fulfill his dream of conquering it. Scott's plans became more urgent when it was learned that the Americans Robert Peary and Matthew Henson with their Eskimo guides had made it to the North Geographic Pole on April 6, 1909. This left the South Geographic Pole as the last major geographic conquest on earth.

Others were interested in this prize, too, including American, German, Japanese, and Scottish expeditions that were either abandoned or failed to reach the continent. Another contestant was the Norwegian, Roald Amundsen, who was leading an expedition to the North Pole when he heard that it had been reached. Amundsen turned around and headed south in hopes of being the first to reach the South Pole.

In England, meanwhile, Scott had faced increasing criticism for the lack of scientific research planned for his expedition, so he decided to reorganize. Two zoologists, a parasitologist, three geologists, two biologists, a physicist, and a meteorologist joined the expedition, as well as a skilled photographer, Herbert Ponting. Consequently, Scott's undertaking became the most scientific to date.

The venture also included the first motor sledges to be taken to Antarctica. Operating on caterpillar tracks, these sledges were Scott's great hope for transportation in reaching the Pole as he distrusted the ability of dogs and ponies in antarctic conditions.

While the expedition's ship, the *Terra Nova*, sailed from London on June 1, 1910, Scott went on ahead on a fast steamer to Cape Town, South Africa, where he later joined the ship before it continued to New Zealand. At Cape Town, Scott received a devastating cable from Roald Amundsen announcing his intentions. But Amundsen didn't say where he intended to make his camp in the Antarctic, which led Scott to believe he would try from the opposite side of the continent from where Scott was to start.

The *Terra Nova* sailed for McMurdo on November 29, 1910, after four weeks of hard preparations in New Zealand. It was a rough journey both for the men and the animals on board. Arriving in McMurdo Sound, Scott selected Cape Evans on Ross Island, a site protected by low hills, to build the base hut. It was about twelve miles from his first camp at Hut Point, which was to be used as a secondary base.

During the landing of supplies, Scott noticed half a dozen killer whales near an ice floe with two dogs staked on it. He called to Ponting, who ran to get a picture. As he did, the whales dived and came up under the ice, breaking it into fragments. Ponting fled to safety, and the dogs were luckily out of the whales' reach. But that day killer whales earned a reputation for diabolical cunning that still persists.

In another incident, one of the motor sledges broke through the ice and sank, inflicting a serious blow to the expedition's optimism.

The *Terra Nova* left Cape Evans and sailed on an exploratory cruise around Ross Island. To their astonishment, the men found Amundsen camped at the Bay of Whales, sixty miles closer to the Pole than Cape Evans. Amundsen had a shore party of nine men and what seemed an unlimited number of dogs, actually 116.

The hospitable English, despite their secret feelings, invited Amundsen aboard for lunch, during which he announced his intent to seek nothing but the Pole.

Scott and the rest of the men were stunned when the ship returned with the news. But Scott decided there was nothing to be done except "to proceed exactly as though nothing had happened."

During the *Terra Nova* cruise, Scott had been laying supply depots while another party led by Griffith Taylor made a geologic survey of the Victoria Land Coast across McMurdo Sound near the Ferrar Glacier. Crossing the Kukri Hills, the men made their way down to discover an ice-free valley, named for Taylor, which contained a four-mile frozen lake.

Winter clamped down on Cape Evans and the Scott expedition kept busy preparing their equipment and making plans for the next season. They celebrated special occasions, including Scott's forty-fourth birthday, and took turns giving lectures about their individual specialties. Ponting, for instance, used slides to present a tour of exotic parts of the world that he had visited.

Among the activities of the winter was the stringing of a telephone line between Cape Evans and Hut Point, establishing the first antarctic communications. But the event of the winter was an arduous trek, which involved crossing Ross Island, by Dr. Wilson, Apsley Cherry-Garrard, and Lieutenant Henry Bowers to study the penguin rookery at Cape Crozier.

In his account of this venture, *The Worst Journey in the World*, Cherry-Garrard tells of the frostbite that plagued them, the nights when it was too cold to keep a hole open in their sleeping bags to breathe, and the mornings when the half-frozen men took four hours to dress and prepare a simple breakfast.

Hut built on Cape Evans, Ross Island, during Robert Scott's second expedition, 1911 U.S. NAVY

It took them nineteen days to reach the emperor rookery where they gathered five eggs and killed three birds for the blubber. They built an igloo for protection on the slopes above the rookery. But strong winds ripped off the canvas roof and the men were forced to lie under snow and rock debris for warmth during a storm. Bowers later wrote that, beneath his debris covering, he pedaled his feet and sang all the songs and hymns he knew to pass the time. He also bumped Wilson to make sure he was alive and to remind him that it was his birthday. Two days later the storm abated and the starving, cold men crawled out.

The party struggled in extremely cold temperatures to Hut Point where some of the expedition were visiting from the main camp. Despite their hardships during the journey, the men had saved three penguin eggs which were later used to prove that penguins were related to the flying birds.

During September and October of 1911, a number of sledging trips were made to establish depots of food and supplies for Scott's southern journey to the Pole and for the second western geological survey to be led by Taylor.

Amundsen, meanwhile, decided to start for the Pole. Taking four men and forty-two dogs, he left the Bay of Whales on October 19, 1911. His plan called for sledging across the ice shelf, up the Axel Heiberg Glacier, and through the Transantarctic Mountains to the polar plateau.

Amundsen's men were expert skiers and dog handlers, which gave him an important edge over Scott. Amundsen also used an insensitive but successful plan to kill a few of his dogs along the way so that his men and the remaining dogs could maintain their strength. At the same time, this allowed him to reduce the amount of food that had to be hauled. The Norwegian also had better luck than Scott in selecting an easier route to the Pole and in starting earlier in the season so that he missed the first winter storms that were eventually to trap Scott.

Scott's plan was to send the motor sledges in advance, followed by the dog teams, and then the main party members with the ponies. The motor sledges started off on October 23 and began having mechanical trouble. In a week they had to be abandoned.

Amundsen (fifth from left) and men work on personal gear. RONALD AMUNDSEN, *The South Pole.* VOL. 1. JOHN MURRAY PUBLISHERS LTD. LONDON, 1912.

The dog teams left Cape Evans on October 31, and the main pony party on November 1. The complete cavalcade consisted of sixteen men, ten ponies, twenty-three dogs, and thirteen sledges.

The ponies suffered miserably pulling the sledges through the increasing soft snow, and they were weakened by periodic blizzards. One by one they had to be killed. On December 9, as the party prepared to ascend the Beardmore Glacier, the five remaining ponies were shot and provided some meat for the dogs and the men. Scott also sent the dog teams back to base at this point. A man-hauling party of twelve then faced the long, hard journey up the Beardmore, following Shackleton's general course.

Sixty-five miles up the glacier, Scott sent back four of the men. He ordered another four to return when the party reached the polar plateau so that only Scott, Wilson, Bowers, Petty Officer Evans, and Army Captain Lawrence Oates struggled on the remaining 168 miles.

As they finally approached their goal on January 16, 1912, they suddenly came on a black flag, with ski and dog tracks running in both directions. They camped and discussed the situation, although it was obvious what had happened.

Amundsen and party camp at the South Pole. SCOTT POLAR RESEARCH
INSTITUTE

The following day they continued to the Pole, made observations, and took photographs. "Great God!" wrote Scott in his diary, "This is an awful place and terrible enough for us to have laboured to it without the reward of priority. . . ."

Starting back on January 18, Scott's party found the spot which the Norwegians had marked as the exact location of the Pole and a record of their arrival there on December 16.

Disappointed and in poor physical condition, the men hauled their sledges toward the Beardmore. An injury to Evans' hand, which he had cut earlier while repairing a sledge runner, was becoming serious. Wilson was suffering from snow blindness and a strained tendon in his leg. The cold seemed to bother Oates more than the others, and his feet eventually turned black from frostbite. Then Scott fell heavily and hurt his shoulder, so that the sturdy, short Bowers was the only really sound member of the party.

They stopped despite their condition to make geological surveys, including one of the coal seams in the magnificient Beacon

80

sandstone cliffs bordering the Beardmore valley, where they collected thirty-five pounds of precious specimen rock.

By this time—January 25—Amundsen had returned to his ship without difficulty. In order to keep to the schedule he had established before his departure, he had had to slow down at times during his return. In spite of plenty of time and opportunity, he did not explore any area on the way or make maps for future use. He consequently spent the rest of his life trying to justify his race to the Pole, whereas Scott became the romantic hero.

Scott and his men continued to struggle down the Beardmore. Four days after leaving the midway depot on the glacier, Evans collapsed and became unconscious. Although the biggest and strongest of the men, he didn't recover and died on February 18. His death was an unhappy relief to the others who had been delayed because of nursing him.

The four survivors made it down the glacier and onto the Ross Ice Shelf. But the winter was beginning and the weather was against them, alternating between blizzards and surface conditions that made the traverse difficult. Oates, with badly frostbitten feet, began to hinder their progress. When they camped to wait out a blizzard on March 16, Oates told them, "I am just going outside and may be some time." He left the tent and never returned.

The others were completely worn out and could advance only

Scott's party pulls sledge across the polar plateau. This picture by Bowers shows (left to right) Evans, Oates, Wilson, and Scott. SCOTT
POLAR RESEARCH INSTITUTE

eighteen miles during the three days after Oates' sacrifice. Then, within eleven miles of their main supply depot, another blizzard struck, trapping them for three days. They were only 160 miles from Hut Point, but hopelessly stranded.

On March 29 Scott made the last entry in the diary he had carried throughout the expedition: "It seems a pity but I do not think I can write more. Last Entry. For God's sake look after our people." As the others lay dying, Scott, in a final burst of energy, opened his sleeping bag and threw his arm across them.

Eight months later, after the winter was over, a rescue party found the three men and Scott's diary. They dug out the sledge and recovered all the gear, including the thirty-five pounds of important geological specimens that Wilson had insisted the party carry to the end. A burial service was read and a large cairn built above the bodies, with a rough cross made from two skis on top. A record of the event was placed in a metal cylinder.

For the next two days the rescue party searched for Oates' body. Deciding it must have been covered by snow, they built another cairn and on it placed a cross and a record of his death.

In January, 1913, when the *Terra Nova* returned to bring the rest of the expedition home, a nine-foot cross was built. It still stands on the summit of Observation Hill, overlooking McMurdo and the Ross Ice Shelf. In addition to the names of the polar party, Cherry-Garrard suggested an epitaph from Tennyson's poem "Ulysses" which has inspired all those who followed Scott to the Antarctic: "To Strive, To Seek, To Find, And Not To Yield."

Two Veterans Return

Douglas Mawson returned to the Antarctic in 1911 as leader of the Australasian Antarctic Expedition. Between 1911 and 1914, his party established bases in King George V Land, Queen Mary Land, and offshore on Macquarie Island. They charted over seven hundred miles of new coastline by sledge and ship.

Mawson was the first to take an airplane to Antarctica, a Vickers monoplane that had been adapted for cold weather while Mawson was fund raising in his native Australia. The plane, however, was not successful and Mawson ordered the wing to be sawn off and the landing gear replaced by runners. However, the

Sir Ernest Shackleton
SCOTT POLAR RESEARCH INSTITUTE

engine failed while hauling supplies between the supply ship and the base camp.

Mawson added his name to the list of heroic explorers during a trip to the interior of 250 miles over previously unseen areas. After the deaths of his two companions, he endured a journey alone back to his coastal base. In his account of the ordeal, he tells how the thickened skin on the soles of his feet flapped loose in a separate layer, exposing raw skin underneath. At one point he fell into a crevasse and hung there in a harness at the end of a rope attached to his sledge, jammed at the edge of the pit. With great effort, he managed to pull himself out and continue.

Shackleton also returned to the Antarctic as the leader of another major expedition. This time, in 1914, he had a scheme to cross the continent from the Weddell Sea to the Ross Sea via the South Geographic Pole. Since both poles had been reached, the transantarctic crossing was one of the few remaining conquests left to be made. He was determined to succeed where others had failed. Fortunately, the Admiralty also supported the venture and commanded he set sail from England despite the outbreak of World War I four days before the date set for departure.

Shackleton's plan was to sail to the coast of the Weddell Sea, from where he would lead the main party across the continent. Meanwhile, a support party, leaving from Tasmania, would establish a base on Ross Island. They would make food and fuel depots across the Ross Ice Shelf for the main party to use during the last leg of its trek.

Trouble plagued this expedition like no other in antarctic history. The support party went to work while its ship, serving as the party's headquarters, anchored in McMurdo Sound near Cape Evans. As the sun was disappearing in April, 1915, four of the men were using Scott's old hut at Cape Evans while the other six members were away laying the depots across the Ross Ice Shelf.

After a storm, the four men looked out of Scott's hut and found their ship, the *Aurora*, gone. When it didn't return, they believed it had sunk. The *Aurora*, however, had been blown out to sea, where it became surrounded by pack ice and drifted helplessly north. The men in the hut had little food, except what Scott's expedition had left behind, and very little fuel for cooking or melting snow for drinking and washing. They had only the clothing they wore, which soon was tattered, greasy, and black.

Little did the support party realize that disaster had also struck the main party. On January 15 of that year, Shackleton's ship, the *Endurance*, had become frozen in the pack ice of the Weddell Sea. The ship and its company of twenty-eight men drifted more than five hundred miles in the ice. Finally, they were forced to abandon the ship, which was crushed and eventually sank on November 21, 1915. The expedition drifted north on the ice for nearly five months. One hundred miles from the South Shetland Islands, they reached open water and took to the small boats they had saved from the *Endurance*.

The group landed on desolate Elephant Island, April 15, 1916. A week later, Shackleton and five men left in one of the boats for the 800-mile trip to South Georgia Island, where they hoped to get help from whalers. In one of the greatest feats of seamanship, they sailed the roughest seas in the world around the tip of South America.

In two weeks Shackleton and his party made it to South Georgia Island, but they landed on the wrong side of the island. Shackleton and three others were forced to make a perilous three-day trek across the mountainous island to the whaling station. There, a rescue party was organized and sailed around the island to pick up the other three men.

Those left on Elephant Island eventually were rescued by a Chilean tug on August 30, after almost five months of hardship.

HMS Endurance *trapped in the ice of the Weddell Sea*   HURLEY, NA-
TIONAL LIBRARY OF AUSTRALIA

Amazingly, none of the main party were lost during the entire incredible adventure.

The support party at Cape Evans, however, didn't fare as well. After the first winter, the group began on October 1, 1915, to try the nearly impossible task of laying the depots they believed Shackleton was counting on. Although suffering with scurvy and exhaustion, six men finished the job on January 26, 1916. One man died from the scurvy during their return across the ice shelf. The other five reached Hut Point and forced their way into Scott's hut there. They waited for the sea to freeze so they could continue to Cape Evans and join the others. Two of the men became impatient, including the expedition leader, Aeneas Mackintosh. The two tried to make it to Cape Evans and were lost during a blizzard. On July 15, the three survivors made the sledge trip safely to the Cape Evans hut.

During the winter the group survived by killing seals and scrounging bits and pieces from the Scott expedition stores. When the sun returned in August, they made some sledging trips, including one to search for Mackintosh and his companion. On January 10, 1917, the scarecrow-looking band, after being stranded nearly two years, suddenly saw the *Aurora* sailing toward them. They rushed across the ice to meet a party from the ship led by Shackleton, who had spent months convincing the English authorities, involved in World War I, to rescue the men at Cape Evans.

THE AIR AGE

The next era in antarctic exploration heralded aviators, beginning with the Australian Hubert Wilkins who made the first airplane flight while leading a private expedition to the Antarctic Peninsula in November of 1928. The pilot, Carl Eielson, was an American with experience flying in Alaska.

From Deception Island, Wilkins flew across the Peninsula, making important geographical observations. In 1928 and 1930 he also tried unsuccessfully to fly across the continent from the Weddell Sea to the Ross Sea. But his flights helped to demonstrate the value of the airplane for survey and reconnaissance work in Antarctica. Aerial photographs taken by Wilkins appeared to show that the Peninsula was separated from the continent by a series of ice-filled channels.

More than Wilkins, it was Richard E. Byrd of the United States Navy who proved the usefulness of the airplane in Antarctica, initiating one of the greatest developments in the exploration of the continent.

Two years before his first antarctic expedition, Byrd claimed to have flown with pilot Floyd Bennett over the North Pole on May 9, 1926, for which he was awarded the Congressional Medal of Honor.

In 1928, Byrd took a biplane to the Antarctic as part of the largest and best equipped expedition to sail to the continent up to that time. On November 29, 1929, Byrd and his crew became the first men to fly over the South Geographic Pole.

As significant as his conquest of the Pole by air were Byrd's aerial exploration of hundreds of miles of unseen antarctic territory, made from his base, Little America, at the Bay of Whales. Two high mountain ranges, the Ford Range and the Rockefeller Mountains, were named for wealthy financial backers. Beyond the mountains, one of the major segments of antarctic territory

Crew prepare the "Floyd Bennett," a Ford tri-motored plane, used by Richard Byrd, Bernt Balchen, Harold June, and Ashley McKinley in their flight over the South Pole. U.S. NAVY

was named Marie Byrd Land after his wife.

Byrd's second expedition (1933–1935) concentrated on scientific work, particularly the mapping of the areas he had discovered earlier. He also used tracked vehicles more extensively than ever before. Among other things, aerial photographs taken by the expedition proved that a channel joining the Ross and Weddell seas was a myth.

At 123 miles south of Little America II, an advance weather station was established where Byrd stayed alone from March 28 through August 10, 1934. No one previously had endured the winter alone or had lived so far inland. During the winter, carbon monoxide fumes from a faulty stove and from the engine that powered his radio nearly killed him. Byrd made radio contact with his base three times a week, but tried to conceal his situation. When his messages became erratic, a party was sent to rescue him.

Byrd's skill as a navigator was only one of his outstanding qualities. He was prominent in developing instruments that made polar flights possible, and he brought to Antarctica modern machines and radio communication for field work.

Two other famous polar explorers were at work in the Antarctic

In 1947, Rear Admiral Richard Byrd enjoys his twelve-year-old pipe at Little America camp. U.S. NAVY

Lincoln Ellsworth U.S. NAVY

with ship and plane at the same time as Byrd. One was Hjalmar Riiser-Larson, who had been on the first transarctic crossing with Amundsen and Lincoln Ellsworth in 1926. Riiser-Larson made several exploratory flights over Antarctica's Princess Ragnhild Coast during 1930-31 and surveyed a range of ice-crystal mountains, over two miles high and luminously blue, which extended for over one hundred miles.

The other explorer was Douglas Mawson, who once again led an expedition to Antarctica. Mawson discovered by air the Mac-Robertson Coast and explored 2500 miles of coastline.

By the end of 1931, consequently, little of the vast coastline remained unexplored. But most of the interior, an area as large as North America, was still unknown. This situation enticed the multimillionaire adventurer Lincoln Ellsworth, who had financed the first transarctic crossing.

Altogether, Ellsworth made four privately financed expeditions to Antarctica. After two unsuccessful attempts, Ellsworth finally gained his goal with Canadian pilot Herbert Hollick-Kenyon. On November 22, 1935, the two men took off from Dundee Island near the tip of the Antarctic Peninsula and flew across the continent to the Bay of Whales. They made four landings during the flight and discovered the Eternity and Sentinel mountain ranges, part of which is Vinson Massif (16,860 feet), the highest point on the continent. The area, Ellsworth Land, was named for Ellsworth's father.

On this final expedition, Ellsworth and his pilot explored the opposite side of the continent, an area later called the American Highland. Ellsworth claimed a total of 300,000 square miles of antarctic territory for the United States, which, however, didn't pursue those claims. Much of the area that Ellsworth explored is now claimed by other countries. But the work of Ellsworth clearly demonstrated that aircraft, taking off and landing on unprepared surfaces, could be used for inland exploration.

More Expeditions

Expeditions from Australia, Britain, and New Zealand contributed important scientific work during this period of aviation conquest. Almost every year, the British Discovery Committee sent a ship to study the seas and marine life in Antarctica. The British hoped to learn enough about whales to save the great mammals from the kind of destruction experienced by fur seals a century earlier. These groups sighted land, made important maps, and assisted other national expeditions.

Whalers continued to make discoveries during this period, too, particularly the family of Norwegian Lars Christensen, who combined the profitable business of whaling with exploration. His factory ships carried airplanes to search for whales and to explore coastal areas as well. In the course of a series of expeditions between 1928 and 1938, Christensen ships, with the aid of the airplanes, explored the coasts of Enderby Land and the neighboring sector which was named Dronning Maud Land for the queen of Norway.

90

The wife of one of the ship's captains, Caroline Mikkelsen, is believed to have been the first woman to go ashore in the Antarctic. She landed in a small boat on February 20, 1935.

Byrd returned briefly to Antarctica as official leader of the United States Antarctic Service Expedition of 1939–41. Pack ice prevented the expedition's two ships from reaching the planned destination and an alternative site was chosen on Stonington Island at the base of the Peninsula.

After supervising the unloading, Byrd returned to the United States with both ships in March of 1940, leaving Richard Black in command and Finn Ronne as chief of staff. The party lived in tents while prefabricated buildings were erected to establish East Base. Today the unoccupied station is the oldest United States base still standing in the Antarctic. Some scientists and historians would like to see it restored and preserved as an historic landmark.

From East Base the expedition carried out extensive aerial mapping of the area, and among its sledging journeys was one of the longest in antarctic history, made by Ronne and Carl Eklund. They covered 1260 miles and collected a variety of scientific data during the 84-day trip.

WORLD WAR II

During the second world war, Adolf Hitler sent Dr. Alfred Ritscher to Enderby Land and Dronning Maud Land to establish a German claim to antarctic territory. Ritscher's aerial survey named mountains and inlets after Nazis and claimed 600,000 square miles of the region. Afterward, the area was bombed with metal swastikas so no one would have any doubt who owned it. Hitler later claimed all of Antarctica when he occupied Norway because of Amundsen's discovery of the South Pole.

Except for this madness, the war only came as close to the continent as the offshore seas where Nazi commerce raiders attacked Allied shipping. Because of the Nazi threat, British warships kept the northern area of the Peninsula under surveillance. The British also built a number of stations on the Peninsula and at one time used the abandoned East Base of the United States.

In 1947, Ronne returned to East Base with a privately financed expedition that was plagued with troubles at the outset. About half of the forty-three huskies died of distemper during the trip south. So the expedition stopped twice in South America seeking replacements, which included a corgi, a whippet, and some sort of sheepdog! They also picked up what they thought were two llamas for their planned surface travel on the Ice. The llamas, however, turned out to be alpacas and were killed by the dogs during the journey. There were also chickens aboard the ship, which must have appeared to be a small version of the Ark.

Ronne arrived to find East Base ransacked. Believing the nearby British expedition was responsible, he restricted social contact with it. The leaders of the two expeditions eventually reconciled their differences over the damages, the United States occupation of British-claimed territory, and the sharing of the only outhouse. They realized that neither could accomplish much without the other. The British had competent dog teams and the Americans had the only aircraft, a twin-engine Beechcraft. So they agreed on a joint exploration that enabled them to map a generally-unknown area of the continent larger than Texas. The world's second largest ice shelf, located on the eastern coast of the Peninsula, was named for Ronne.

Ronne's expedition included two women, his wife, Edith, and Jenny Darlington, wife of the second man in command. They became the first women to winter-over in Antarctica.

When the expedition was ready to leave in February of 1948, they were unable to blast their ship free of the sea ice. For assistance, Ronne radioed two icebreakers that he knew were passing by as part of "Operation Highjump," a new United States expedition. Ronne was reluctant to ask for help until Mrs. Darlington reported she was several months pregnant with the first child known to be conceived in Antarctica. (It wasn't until 1978 that the first baby, an Argentine boy, was born on the continent.)

The icebreakers freed Ronne's ship and continued on to take part in the largest expedition ever sent to the continent. Commanded jointly by Byrd and Richard Cruzen, Operation Highjump included four thousand men and thirteen ships. During

1946, while Ronne had been planning his expedition, Little America IV was set up at the Bay of Whales as the operational base camp. In 1947, seaplanes and land-based aircraft mapped 537,000 square miles (nearly 60 per cent) of the continent's coastline. About one-quarter of this had never been seen before. More of Antarctica was explored during this expedition than ever before.

On a visit to Scott's hut at Cape Evans, Byrd's men found cans, bones, and the frozen carcass of a dog standing up as though alive. The most surprising discovery of Operation Highjump was a so-called oasis on the Knox Coast of Wilkes Land. Blue and green ice-free lakes were found scattered among three hundred square miles of bare, brown hills. The lakes were later determined to be inner arms of the sea.

THE IGY

Current scientific study in Antarctica resulted from the International Geophysical Year (IGY) of 1957–58, when scientists made an all-out effort to learn more about all parts of the world, including Antarctica. During the IGY, twelve nations mounted huge logistical efforts to establish fifty-five observatories on the continent and offshore islands. Scientific parties for the first time were based on the polar plateau.

A great amount of work went into planning the IGY, most of which was highly cooperative. But at one stage the United States and the Soviet Union nearly clashed over a dramatic proposal by the United States to build a permanent station at the South Geographic Pole, an important strategic position in the eyes of the Soviets. Disagreement was avoided when the Soviets decided to build Vostok Station and two others in scientifically important areas of the vast interior.

The logistics involved in building the stations of the IGY marked many historic milestones. For the first time, aircraft from a distant land mass took off and landed on the continent when two standard C-54s and two ski-equipped P2V Neptunes flew from New Zealand to McMurdo Station on December 20, 1955. The trip, taking fourteen and one-half hours, inaugurated the first Operation Deep Freeze, during which the McMurdo facility was constructed. These planes also made a series of flights over two million square miles of Antarctica, half of which had never been seen before.

A second United States station, Little America V, was set up that year at Kainan Bay near the Bay of Whales. In his farewell to the Antarctic, Admiral Byrd attended the formal opening ceremony. He died the following year.

During 1956–57, in the final season before the actual start of the IGY, the United States undertook the formidable task of establishing a station in Marie Byrd Land by hauling components in a tractor train from Little America V. The outpost at the South Pole was built by airlifting men and materials by eight Air Force C-124 Globemasters from McMurdo. A month before the work began, the commander of Deep Freeze II, Admiral George Dufek, flew in an R-4D to the Pole to review the site and to ensure the Soviets hadn't gotten there first.

The Soviet Union, whose sole interest in Antarctica since the voyage of Bellingshausen had been confined to whaling, had sent its first comprehensive expedition to the continent in November of 1955. After building an observation station on the Knox Coast (Mirny), the Soviets established three outposts along a 1250-mile route inland, the last of which was Vostok Station. It took them two years to complete the entire program.

Rear Admiral Richard Byrd salutes the raising of the Flag at the South Pole, 1955. Beside him to the right is Dr. Paul Siple.

U.S. NAVY

But the most important aspect of this operation was the way in which the Soviet scientists cooperated with their Australian hosts in this sector of Antarctica which was claimed by Australia, even though Australian sovereignty wasn't recognized by the Soviets. The veteran explorer Sir Douglas Mawson extended a warm welcome to the Russians and they in turn opened their installations to inspection by Australians from neighboring bases. A regular exchange of meteorological data between the two expeditions was also organized.

Soon all kinds of scientific information was freely flowing between the Soviets and all the nations active in the IGY. Soviet scientists were being exchanged with those of other Western nations, an unprecedented measure at a time when the Soviet Union and the United States were engaged in the "cold war."

The IGY was successful from a scientific standpoint, too. Great sunspot activity and one of the greatest magnetic storms recorded in history occurred, as the scientists had hoped at the start of the program. Weather reports from stations throughout the continent were gathered at Little America V. Men from several nations interpreted the reports and drew up weather charts for the entire Antarctic for the first time.

Much of the limelight of the IGY, however, was stolen by the first overland crossing of the continent. The four-month journey was led by Vivian Fuchs of the United Kingdom, following a plan similar to Shackleton's. The main party, led by Fuchs, traveled from the Weddell Sea to the Ross Sea via the South Pole. A support party, headed by Edmund Hillary (the New Zealander who conquered Mount Everest), laid depots of food and fuel on the Ross Ice Shelf and the polar plateau for the final stage of Fuch's crossing. While laying the depots, Hillary and his men traveled all the way to the Pole. They became the first men since Scott to have reached the Pole overland when they arrived on January 4, 1958.

Fuchs completed the transantarctic crossing on March 2 when he arrived at McMurdo. His men made seismic soundings and gravity measurements across Antarctica to determine the depth of the ice and discovered that most of the land under the ice cap was above sea level. They also helped to establish that Antarctica was indeed a continent, not a group of mountainous islands covered by ice.

THE ANTARCTIC TREATY

The IGY was scheduled to end in 1958 but the value of the scientific findings convinced most of the nations to stay on. Because of the likelihood of permanent occupation, the nations drew up a treaty to ensure the continuation of the international cooperation established during the IGY.

Meeting in Washington, D.C., twelve countries agreed to the Antarctic Treaty in December of 1958, and it became effective in 1961. The original signators were Argentina, Australia, Belgium, Chile, France, Japan, New Zealand, Norway, South Africa, the Soviet Union, the United Kingdom, and the United States. Czechoslovakia, Poland, Denmark, Brazil, the Netherlands, and the German Democratic Republic have since joined.

The signators suspended all territorial claims for ten years and agreed to prevent Antarctica from being used for military purposes or for the disposal of nuclear wastes. Information would be shared and installations open for inspection at all times. The United States and the Soviet Union made no claims to territory but, as mentioned before, neither did they recognize the claims of other countries. Both reserved the right to make future claims based on the activities of their citizens on the continent.

The Antarctic Treaty was a landmark document because it created confidence among the countries of the world. It later served as the model for the Test Ban Treaty of 1963, the Space Agreement of 1967, and the Nuclear Non-proliferation Pact of 1968.

SINCE THE IGY

Many of the stations built during the IGY have been improved, changed to different locations, or abandoned. Some, such as McMurdo and Vostok, remain and their importance for scientific and logistical operations has not altered.

Another significant change has been the inclusion of women in

Accompanied by Rear Admiral D. F. Welch, the first women arrive at the South Pole. U.S. NAVY

the expeditions after years of male resistance. The United States sent the first women scientists to Antarctica in 1969. Led by Dr. Lois Jones, the Ohio State University team included Eileen Mc-Saveney, Kay Lindsay, and Terry Tickhill. Living out of tents, the women studied the frozen lakes and glaciers receding up the barren walls of the ice-free valleys discovered by Griffith Taylor during Scott's second expedition. Every ten days a helicopter ferried the women to McMurdo Station where they could use the science laboratory, do their laundry, and take a shower.

In November of 1969 they were joined by Pam Young, a scientist with the New Zealand Antarctic Research Program that year, and Jean Pearson, a science writer for the *Detroit News*, on a flight to the South Pole. When the Herc landed, they joined arms with the commander of Deep Freeze and together stepped off the lowered tail ramp of the plane, becoming the first women to visit the Pole.

Since 1969, women scientists have worked at various sites on the Ice. Women have also wintered-over and headed groups of all-male research assistants. In addition, women have been assigned to non-scientific roles in support of the research program, including working in the kitchen. Antarctica, once the all-male bastion. finally has been conquered by women.

97

4. Unlocking the Frozen Secrets

THE ICE SHEET

Because the signators continue to adhere to the Antarctic Treaty, the continent so far has remained the vast, natural laboratory created by the IGY. Antarctica continues to hold special interest for scientists because of its size, location, and unusual features.

Ice is the most obvious of these scientific interests. Antarctica is blanketed with 95 per cent of all the permanent ice in the world. The North Pole region, by contrast, is a sea covered with drifting ice floes only a few feet thick. The only substantial ice sheet there covers Greenland.

The mean thickness of the south polar ice cap is more than 6000 feet, making the ice-covered continent the highest of all in elevation. In eastern Antarctica, 350 miles south of Australia's Casey Station, the ice reaches a height of 15,800 feet.

So much ice forces the land underneath it below sea level. If this weight were removed, the land would rise. The resulting meltwater would swell the seas around the world by 250 feet, causing extensive flooding. Scientists believe such an increase in the oceans occurred when the northern ice sheet retreated during the Pleistocene Epoch.

Although the ice in Antarctica is said to be permanent, it is a

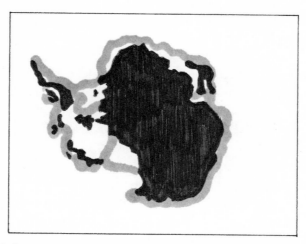

Dark shaded areas represent the land beneath the antarctic ice cap.

W. CALDWELL

constantly changing force that influences the levels of the seas around the globe, even today. The ice actually consists of many layers of varying thickness that are constantly moving at different rates of speed. Pressure from the weight of the ice itself causes this movement. As a result, glaciers, "rivers of ice," press out from the high center of the continent toward the sea.

Scientists have long studied the factors that control the flow of

Exposed land areas not covered by the ice cap   W. CALDWELL

99

glacier ice toward the sea. Some glaciers, they have found, are slow, and some are fast. Others remain almost stagnant until there is a critical level of ice accumulation; then they surge, moving rapidly to sea. The Beardmore Glacier that flows into the Ross Ice Shelf, for instance, is the swiftest and thickest. Like the central current of a river, the center flows more rapidly (about three feet daily) than the sides, which move very little.

Scientists believe the surges of antarctic ice happen in cycles, about every few tens of thousands of years. (Such a surge is thought to have cleared ice from central Canada eight thousand years ago.) If this speculation is right, eastern Antarctica is just beginning to recover from its last ice surge, whereas western Antarctica reached its maximum ice thickness two thousand years ago and now is nearing the stage of slipping into the Pacific Ocean.

Such a massive discharge of the antarctic ice into the oceans would have a devastating effect on the rest of the world. If a substantial part of the ice slipped into the sea, it would spread to cover a large part of the southern oceans. Its snowy surface would reflect so much solar energy back into space that the entire earth's atmosphere would be cooled, starting an ice age. In addition, the immediate effect of such a vast quantity of ice surging into the water would be massive tidal waves that could completely wreck coastal regions even in the Northern Hemisphere.

As part of the information about past and future ice ages, scientists have found that massive ice sheets once flowed out in all directions from such areas as Canada, Scandinavia, and the Soviet Union, in addition to Antarctica. Some scientists argue that this indicates much of the world's water was locked into ice sheets during the ice ages. This would have lowered the seas, making possible new islands and land bridges between continents, by which animals and people may have migrated from one place to another.

Whereas some scientists predict a new ice age in future, others maintain that man's environmental interference has halted its approach. Professor David M. Gates of the University of Michigan told the 1977 meeting of the American Institute of Biological

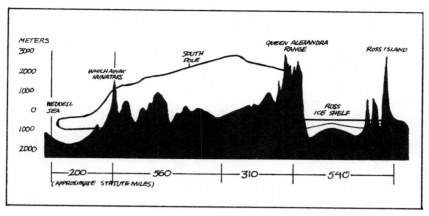

A cross section of the antarctic continent indicates the shape of the land underneath the ice cap. NATIONAL SCIENCE FOUNDATION

Sciences that future increases of carbon dioxide in the atmosphere, caused by burning fossil fuels, will create a warmer global climate. Leading Soviet scientists made a similar forecast in 1971 when they said the polar ice would melt in about two hundred years and flood the major ports of the world because man's increased activities are heating up the atmosphere.

GIANT ICEBERGS

Today, Antarctica relentlessly sends an arsenal of icebergs northward, making the seas extremely dangerous for shipping near the continent. Some of these icebergs are gigantic, such as one almost as large as Rhode Island that apparently broke off from the Princess Martha Coast in 1967. Measuring twenty-five by forty-five miles in size, the iceberg drifted around the Weddell Sea for ten years before colliding with the Larsen Ice Shelf on the eastern rim of the Antarctic Peninsula and dislodging another iceberg, thirteen by thirty-six miles in area.

According to the National Aeronautics and Space Administration, (NASA), both icebergs were monitored by satellite photographs in 1977 to make certain they broke up and melted before they could enter shipping lanes in the Southern Hemisphere. NASA also estimated that the larger of the icebergs contained enough fresh water to supply California's needs (at 1977 levels)

101

Tabular iceberg floats away from the continent.   U.S. NAVY

for years, assuming none of the ice melted on the way there.

Giant icebergs have been sighted before in the Antarctic. For instance, in 1926 the Norwegian whalers aboard the ship *Odd I* reported seeing a berg 100 miles long. Soviet seamen in 1965 said they saw one off Enderby Land that was 87 miles long and 2700 square miles in area.

The idea of using antarctic icebergs for fresh water in other parts of the world is not as farfetched as many would imagine. In 1977, the Saudi Arabian government hired a reputable French engineering group to determine the practicality of towing antarctic icebergs of "moderate" size to the Red Sea to relieve water shortages in that desert area.

According to the French company, Cicero, icebergs weighing eighty-five million tons would be towed over a distance of five thousand miles through the Indian Ocean and the Red Sea. The icebergs would be hauled one at a time by six powerful tugboats, usually used to tow oil-drilling platforms at sea. Cruising at about one knot, the boats would take six months to a year to make the journey from Antarctica. A plastic wrapping, eighteen inches thick, would be used to protect the iceberg against water, waves, and sun so that no more than 20 per cent of it would be lost.

Because of the narrow entrance to the Red Sea, the icebergs would have to be sliced up into smaller pieces by thermal drilling. When the slices finally arrived at Jidda, Saudi Arabia, melting could take up to eighteen months. On top of each iceberg slice, lakes would form from the melted ice. This water would then be pumped through a floating pipeline into reservoirs ashore.

The French engineers believe the plan, estimated at ninety million dollars, would be economical because it would cost twice as much to desalt water from the sea.

Both the United States and Australia have studied similar projects to provide water to desert areas in Southern California and the interior of the Australian continent. But this speculation has never developed to the planning stage.

In addition to their size, antarctic icebergs have other fascinating aspects. Most, for example, are glistening white. However, black-and-white icebergs, made up of dark and light ice, have also been sighted. Bottle-green icebergs are believed to contain fine rock materials such as iron, copper, or other metals that give the icebergs their appearance of color. On the other hand, microorganisms attached to the surface of an iceberg can cause it to look red or brown.

DRILLING THE ICE CAP

Among other things, debris trapped in the ice reveals how weather has changed in the past, thus helping to predict future long-term variations in the climate of the world. Throughout history, the ice has built up a frozen record of matter, including pollen, dust, volcanic ash, and meteorites from outer space. A cross-section sample of the ice layers can tell much about conditions at the time the ice was formed, much as the rings of a tree reveal its age and past events that have effected it.

To reveal the layers of trapped particles in the antarctic ice cap, scientists have drilled deep holes into it and carefully extracted ice core samples. They have been able to measure the decay of various radio-active isotopes to determine the age and other properties of the ice cores.

In 1968, scientists attempted to make the first drilling to the bottom of the ice sheet. The Americans reached bottom near Byrd Station at a depth of 7100 feet. But only a few samples of the soil below could be brought up before the drill froze in the

Researcher checks ice core samples.   T. MASON

hole and became warped by the movement of the relentless ice.

The project at Byrd Station was abandoned, although some important information was gained, including the existence of a slushy layer of ice deep within the ice cap. This discovery was backed up by British scientists flying across the continent in United States Hercs to probe the ice with radar. They found numerous "lakes" beneath the ice. Such findings suggest that the antarctic ice may indeed be getting ready to "surge" en masse into the oceans. Heat flowing up from within the earth has formed a lubricating slush on which the upper layers of ice could slip into the seas.

On the opposite side of the continent from Byrd Station, the Soviets in 1975 succeeded in drilling two holes through the apron of shelf ice attached to the Princess Astrid Coast of Queen Maud Land. One drilling penetrated 1171 feet of ice at a point 22 miles from the edge bordering the sea. The other hole, drilled thirty miles from the ice edge, reached 1466 feet. Bottom sediment was obtained from the sea underneath the ice for the Soviets to study.

United States engineers in December of 1977 succeeded in drilling through the Ross Ice Shelf to reach the "lost world" of the hidden sea underneath. The year before they had been thwarted three hundred feet short of their goal. Ice flowed around the conventional drill assembly during a crew change and locked the drill in place.

Using a newly developed 25-foot, rocket-like torch, the engineers blasted the new hole 10 inches to 2 feet wide through the floating ice shelf at a point where it is 1375 feet thick. Although the shaft started to freeze before researchers from six countries could begin work, a heating cable previously installed enabled them to melt it open.

A television camera lowered through the hole to the seabed revealed something swimming in waters that have been cut off from sunlight and air for perhaps millions of years. The scientists later let down traps to catch any specialized forms of life unseen before and devices to gather samples of sediment and rocks from the sea bottom. Analysis of the sea floor and ice cores taken from the drill hole provide clues to past geologic climate and glacial history, including the question of whether sections of the inland ice periodically slip rapidly into the ocean, raising sea levels worldwide.

The scientists also saw signs of life in the form of tracks, trails, and burrows on the sea bottom. The water beneath the drill site, 470 miles southeast of McMurdo Station, is about 660 feet deep. It is not entirely isolated because of currents that link it to the Ross Sea and the Pacific Ocean.

Ice core samples from antarctic drill holes, in addition to those from other glacier regions, are stored at the State University of New York at Buffalo. Observations made by scientists at the drill site are checked for accuracy, and this information is placed in a computerized data bank. What remains of the ice core is stored. The ice core data and samples of the ice core are made available on request to the National Science Foundation so that other scientists can study them.

In addition to drilling, scientists use radar-soundings to study the ice cap and what lies below it. They have found mountain ranges to be more extensive than previously believed, as well as the lakes in the ice layers mentioned earlier. One research project recently involved the cooperation of five nations. While the United States and Britain were making radar-sounding flights across eastern Antarctica, Australia, France, and the Soviet Union conducted overland traverses by tracked vehicles. The information they gathered has been put together to produce a better picture of the various layers of ice and the land underneath them.

THE CLIMATE

The most surprising aspect of the antarctic climate is its great variation, which is due to the huge size of the continent. The average temperature at the South Geographic Pole is −60° Fahrenheit, while the Antarctic Peninsula averages 26° Fahrenheit. Most coastal areas, however, have a mean temperature of about zero degrees, with summer temperatures sometimes reaching above the freezing mark. The average temperature for all of Antarctica is −34° Fahrenheit.

The lowest temperature recorded was in 1960 at Vostok Station when the thermometer plummeted to −126.9° Fahrenheit. Temperatures nearly as cold have been recorded at Amundsen-Scott South Pole Station.

In addition to being cold, the climate is extremely dry. Each year less than three inches of water-equivalent in the form of snow falls at the South Pole, making it drier than most tropical

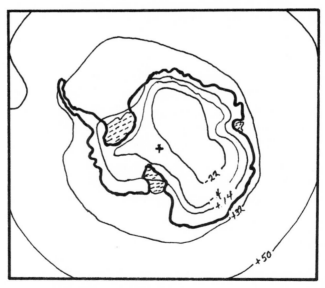

Antarctic summer temperatures—January

NATIONAL SCIENCE FOUNDATION

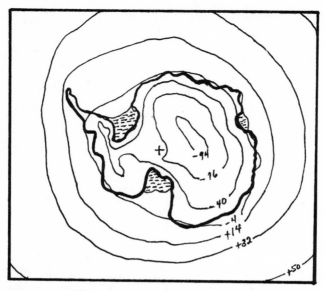

Antarctic winter temperatures—July NATIONAL SCIENCE FOUNDATION

deserts. Coastal areas, being warmer, get more moisture—from eight to twenty-nine inches, but the average is about five inches for the entire continent. Why then does Antarctica have so much ice? The answer is that snow has accumulated for thousands of years and compacted into ice layers.

The antarctic blizzards are different from what they seem to be. Often the blizzards are the result of the winds blowing old snow across the surface, rather than from new snow falling. Antarctic winds are famous for being the worst in the world. The windiest area of all is the coast south of Australia, where gusts of 200 mph have been measured.

The antarctic winds are created by the dome shape of the continent. The air above the high, central plateau cools and becomes heavier as it rushes down to the coast. Accelerating quickly, the wind often attains gale strength by the time it reaches the sea. Sometimes a cyclone passes near the continent, adding its influence in creating hurricane-force winds that can last for days.

Careful attention is paid to the weather in Antarctica because all activity, including life itself, depends on knowing what the weather is going to do. In addition, air around the continent exerts a great effect on the weather in other parts of the Southern

Navyman prepares to launch meteorological balloon.   T. MASON

Hemisphere. (Atmospheric conditions in the rest of the world also influence the polar atmosphere, which is illustrated by the increasing amount of pollution found in the air over Antarctica.)

Balloons and rockets carrying instruments into the atmosphere above Antarctica are launched daily, as well as measurements taken at outposts across the surface. Twice daily two United States satellites beam down pictures of the cloud coverage over the continent.

Various nations, including the United States and Australia, have experimented with automated weather-reporting stations for remote areas. This would reduce the need for long, lonely vigils by scientists collecting data. One such automated geophysical observatory, designed by a Stanford University team, was installed near McMurdo Station in 1972. The observatory's instruments were crammed into a six-foot cylinder mounted atop a fifteen-foot pyramid made of tubular metal. A dish-shaped antenna on top transmitted data gathered by the instruments to orbiting satellites. Powered by a 100-watt battery and a windmill-operated generator, the observatory was designed to transmit data about geomagnetism, cosmic rays, auroral displays, and ionospheric disturbances, as well as the weather.

Scientists hoped to place such automated observatories across Antarctica, thereby cutting the costs of collecting this type of atmospheric information. The unmanned observatories would also speed the processing of data by using satellites to transmit it directly to the United States. Manned stations could then be eliminated in remote spots and the size of other stations reduced.

Unfortunately, the 1200-pound observatory failed to withstand the fierce antarctic climate, including winds of 100 mph. The windmill-powered generator failed, and the project was temporarily abandoned. But it seems almost certain that some type of automated observatories will be used in Antarctica in the future.

Once meteorogolical observations have been made on the Ice, the information is relayed to all other stations so that the data is shared. Reports are also sent to the meteorological center for the Southern Hemisphere in Melbourne, Australia. The Melbourne center provides important information to countries in the South-

Blizzard at a remote spot
U.S. NAVY

ern Hemisphere on how they will be affected by weather patterns approaching from Antarctica.

ATMOSPHERIC STUDIES

In addition to the weather, scientists are interested in other events that occur in the atmosphere over Antarctica. The most exciting are the auroras, called there "the southern lights." Auroras are seen as sudden, violent flashes of color that move across the winter sky. They occur during the summer, too, but are only seen easily when it's dark. The long polar night allows extended periods of observation against a sky that is continuously dark for four and a half months. (Sometimes at the South Pole there are nights when even stars don't appear in the sky due to the position of the earth.)

Auroras are caused, scientists believe, by electrically charged particles emitted by the sun colliding with the gases of the earth's upper atmosphere. These particles are unable to penetrate the earth's magnetic shield at the middle and lower latitudes. But at the polar regions they are able to bombard the atmosphere and produce visible auroral light in the night sky.

Auroras may take the form of bands, rays, arcs, or even draperies of color. They may last several minutes or many hours. A contortion may take place, producing many different-colored

110

forms in the sky. Sometimes the entire sky glows or appears to be in violent motion. You may look up into the night sky and unexpectedly see lights flash on and off, rays shoot and flicker, or bands of color move across the horizon. The eerie displays are often more spectacular than fireworks on the Fourth of July and more fascinating.

Scientists have long been interested in the distribution, depth, composition, and other particulars of the aurora because the particles causing the light are energized before they enter the earth's atmosphere. The source and nature of this energy are still unanswered, challenging questions, although in general it is thought the particles come from the sun.

Cameras that photograph the entire night sky from horizon to horizon are used to record the auroras. Photometers are also used to gather data about visual auroras as well as the "sub-visual" ones that can't be seen by the naked eye. Scientists think the sub-visual or soft auroras are caused by particles of low energy.

The use of satellites has greatly expanded the potential of finding out more about the strange auroras. Particle measurements made by the satellites high in the atmosphere can be compared with auroral levels monitored by photometers on the Ice.

One of the results of studying the auroras is that scientists can determine the composition of the atmosphere around the earth. Each color in an aurora represents a different element present in

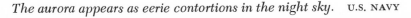

The aurora appears as eerie contortions in the night sky.   U.S. NAVY

the atmosphere. Yellow-green, the most commonly seen, indicates oxygen is present, for instance.

A new project was set up at Siple Station during 1976–77 to study the aurora. Using a fifty-megahertz very high frequency radar system, scientists began studying echoes returned from the part of the atmosphere where auroras occur. They hope this experiment will help them understand the auroral phenomenon in more detail.

The ionosphere is also the playground for low frequency radio noises called "whistlers." These are created by lightning flashes in the atmosphere. They make a whistling sound of descending pitch, a few seconds apart, which can be amplified on a radio receiver so scientists can hear them.

To speed up research, scientists use special radio equipment and the thirteen-mile antenna at Siple Station to create whistlers in the atmosphere when they want them. One day they hope to use this research to control some of the disturbances in the ionosphere that upset radio communications around the world.

Using the VLF transmitter, other upper atmospheric research is conducted at Siple, such as direction-finding experiments carried out in conjunction with a station at Roberval, Canada. The two outposts are called conjugate stations because they are located at opposite ends of one of the magnetic lines of force that emanate around the earth. Because whistlers and other disturbances bounce back and forth along the magnetic lines of force between the poles of the earth, important information can be gained about them by recording observations from spots at opposite ends of the globe. Through these comparative or conjugate studies, scientists can learn more about the atmosphere and the magnetic field that surrounds the earth.

To supplement the information collected by the radio antenna on the ground, scientists at Siple use gigantic 50,000-cubic-foot balloons to carry instruments up to 100,000 feet. They also used three Nike Tomahawk rockets during the 1977–78 season to investigate electron precipitation triggered by very low frequency radio wave emissions in the upper reaches of the atmosphere.

As well as Siple, most stations in Antarctica are the sites of

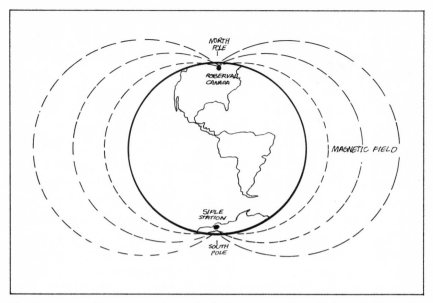

*Conjugate studies are made at Siple Station and at Roberval, Canada,
located at opposite ends of a magnetic line of force.* W. CALDWELL

various research projects to study the upper atmosphere and farther into space. One of the more intriguing projects takes place in
an isolated hut near McMurdo Station. Inside, a mysterious click-
ing sound can be heard as cosmic rays crashing in from outer
space are counted. Cosmic rays are invisible rays of short-wave
length that continuously bombard the earth from deep in space.
Little is known about them except that they have great penetrat-
ing power. Some can even shoot through metal.

The majority of cosmic rays, however, never reach the earth
because the magnetic field surrounding the planet reflects most of
them. But cosmic rays can reach the poles where the magnetic
field curves inward. Because there is no permanent land on which
to build observatories at the North Pole, Antarctica is the best
place on earth to study cosmic rays.

These scientific studies also reveal new knowledge about the
earth's magnetic field as a result of the ways in which it affects
cosmic rays. Scientists seek to answer such questions as how thick
the magnetic field is, whether its size varies from place to place,

113

how much its size fluctuates, and whether its protective shield changes. Some believe that the magnetic field may have changed at times in the past, allowing cosmic rays to strike areas of the earth other than the poles. One theory suggests storms of cosmic rays could have created changes in plants and animals living at such a time. A frog, for instance, could have adapted a different color or skin texture as a result of cosmic ray bombardment.

ROCKS

Despite all the ice, geologists have found that Antarctica has similar kinds of rocks and mountains as other southern continents. The Ellsworth Mountains in Antarctica represent a continuation of the South American Andes, and they also resemble mountains in eastern Argentina. Igneous rocks in the Transantarctic Mountains can be compared with rocks of similar age and composition in Brazil, South Africa, and the Australian island of Tasmania.

Antarctica's volcanoes, such as Mount Erebus, are covered by ice. Most of them have been revealed only by the use of infra-red photography which registers the presence of heat below the ice mantle. Although most are inactive, the volcano on Deception Island off the Peninsula has erupted in recent times, forcing the evacuation of a nearby British station.

One type of rock gives off a radio-active glow when heated, enabling scientists to estimate from the amount of light how long the rocks have been cold. Scientists use these glowing rocks to determine the history of glaciers, which cut the rocks out of the mountain sides when they passed by.

In addition to volcanoes, geologists have discovered "hot" mountains that consist of layers of ice and ash, like multi-layered hot-fudge sundaes, instead of the usual solid rock. These unique mountains have towers of ice between thirty to sixty feet high formed by escaping steam in the cold antarctic air.

"Alien" rocks, meteorites from outer space, have also been found in Antarctica recently. On three expeditions, Japanese scientists discovered thousands of diverse types of meteorites in a small area near Syowa Base, the Japanese antarctic station. They were surprised because only about one meteorite a day is estimated to fall on the earth, including the oceans. Meteorites are hard to find, even when camera networks have recorded their descent to earth.

The scientists believe the reason for finding so many meteorites in one area of Antarctica resulted from the action of the ice. For thousands or perhaps millions of years, ice flowing toward the coast from the high interior was blocked by the coastal mountains. There, the ice was eventually removed by evaporation, sublimation, or wind action. Any meteorites that fell on the ice during its long, slow journey toward the coastal mountains might have accumulated on the surface rather than been buried.

The meteorites found in Antarctica are particularly important because they will help scientists settle the argument about the origin of meteorites. Currently, the scientists debate three theories: the rock fragments are parts of shattered asteroids in space, they are material that condensed as the solar system was forming, or they come from material that existed before the solar system was formed.

Fossils

In certain types of rocks, such as sandstone, researchers and explorers since Shackleton's 1907 expedition have found fossilized remains of plants and animals that prove the frozen continent was once a very different kind of place.

Among the important fossils geologists discovered was the Glossopterid tree, which grew about thirty-three feet high and had large leaves. Because the Glossopterid tree has also been found in Brazil, South Africa, and India, it has provided part of the increasing evidence that the southern lands once were connected.

Extinct amphibians and reptiles also have been uncovered in Antarctica and matched with those discovered in other southern regions. One of these amphibians, the Labyrinthodont, lived about two hundred million years ago.

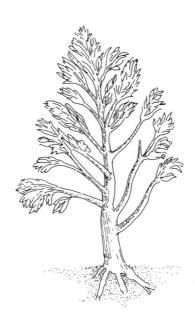

Hypothetical reconstruction of the glossopterid tree W. CALDWELL, AFTER J. RIGBY, *Antarctic Journal of the United States,* MAY–JUNE 1970

The forerunner of the salamander, Labyrinthodonts unfortunately didn't have any internal temperature controls so they couldn't survive great changes of heat and cold. Because they needed a warm climate to stay alive, scientists believe Antarctica once had to have been located in a warmer place.

Before the weather changed and trapped them, such amphibians spent much of their time around wide, shallow lakes where they laid their eggs. The lakes stretched out over the tops of vast lava flows that had erupted through large cracks in the ground. Small fish similar to minnows and larger fish like the garpike lived in the fresh-water lakes of Antarctica during this period.

One of the important reptiles that lived around the lakes was the Lystrosaurus. About the size of a small dog, the Lystrosaurus had a beak-shaped head and two large, protruding teeth. It spent much of its time around water as a hippopotamus does today.

Scientists were elated in 1969 when they discovered the first bones of a Lystrosaurus reptile in Antarctica. These bones matched those already found in Africa and India. The same dry-

116

Lystrosaurus w. CALDWELL AFTER COLBERT, *Age of Reptiles,* w. w. NORTON

land reptile apparently lived in all three places at the same time. Because the Lystrosaurus couldn't swim very well, scientists conclude that Antarctica had to be attached to the other southern continents millions of years ago when this reptile existed.

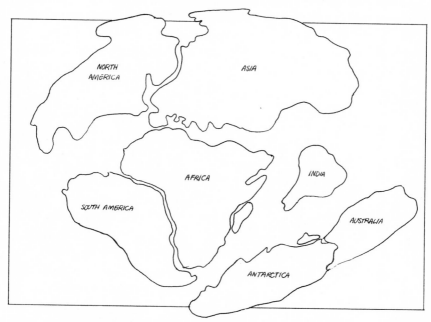

The continents, 200 million years ago, drifting toward their present locations after splitting apart from a single land mass, according to the theory postulated by Alfred Wegener in 1912. w. CALDWELL

The plant and animal fossil discoveries in Antarctica created new interest in the theory of continental drift, first proposed in 1912 by Alfred Wegener. According to his theory, the continents were once part of a single land mass. About two hundred million years ago this land mass split into two large land areas. These areas in turn broke up into the continents which drifted to their present locations and are still moving. If this theory is correct, some time in the distant future the California coast may tear away and drift toward Alaska. Africa and South America may move farther apart and Australia, drifting north, may collide with Asia.

The details of continental drift have not yet been established. Many earth scientists believe the drifting occurs because the earth's crust consists of large, rigid plates that are in continual slow motion. Others think continental movement is caused by spreading of the sea floor along certain points.

Scientists plan during 1977–78 to return to the Fremouw Formation in the central Transantarctic Mountains where the first Lystrosaurus was found. They hope to find more vertebrate fossils that will provide additional evidence to support the theory of continental drift.

Fossilized bones of extinct reptiles discovered in Antarctica prove the continent was once connected to other southern lands. U.S. NAVY

DRY VALLEYS

Since Griffith Taylor discovered them, the ice-free valleys sixty miles west of McMurdo Station continue to pose many intriguing questions for scientists.

These valleys, which cover four thousand square miles, are so dry that the climate can crack your clothing as well as your skin. Researchers find themselves drinking gallons of water to satisfy a terrific thirst. Also, the valleys are so barren that they are like the surface of the moon. Astronauts have visited these valleys as part of their training and tested equipment such as the lunar rover.

The ice-free valleys have aided the space program in other ways, too. Scientists invented very sensitive equipment to detect microscopic animals living in the soil. These life-detecting instruments were used on the space probes that landed on Mars in 1976 and sampled the soil. Like Antarctica, Mars is very cold and dry, but so far scientists haven't found any minute animals there.

Antarctic soil, filled with micro-organisms, was used to test the special laboratory in Houston where astronauts were to be quarantined after returning from the moon. Space officials wanted to ensure that the astronauts didn't bring back any strange, new germs to contaminate the earth. They placed the antarctic soil in the quarantine rooms and waited to see if any of the micro-organisms escaped from it. When none did, the scientists assumed the rooms were tight enough to hold any invisible moon creatures.

Scientists have also found that these antarctic micro-organisms have been around a long time. Holes drilled in the dry valleys have produced cores of frozen ground with micro-organisms ten thousand to one million years old. When these minute life forms were taken to the McMurdo biology lab, they were revived and began to grow when the core sample was warmed!

Algae, bacteria, and fungi microbes also have been discovered living inside rocks strewn about the dry valleys for 200,000 years. When they broke apart samples of the rocks, scientists revealed microbes thriving about one-fortieth of an inch below the surface where sunlight and moisture could reach them.

As well as life in the rocks and soil, scientists have seen algae and fungi growing in the frozen lakes, despite the ice cover-

Biologists study micro-organisms beside Lake Vanda in the dry Wright Valley. NATIONAL SCIENCE FOUNDATION

ing. Lakes such as Lake Vanda have varying warm layers. Five miles long and 217 feet deep, Lake Vanda is permanently covered with ice up to 13 feet thick. Yet the bottom temperature of the lake is over 75° Fahrenheit.

Scientists say Lake Vanda is warm because of its high salt content. The layers of different temperatures are caused by layers of salt water with different densities. Each layer, because of the varying densities, absorbs and retains different amounts of heat from the sun.

Another lake in the region, Lake Bonney, also has layers that differ in their temperature, chemistry, and inhabitants. The lake's maximum depth is one hundred feet and its bottom temperature in summer reaches 45° Fahrenheit. Although the lake is covered with fourteen feet of permanent ice, in late summer an opening of water twenty feet wide forms around its rim. But far stranger things have been happening during the months of continual sunshine.

On the bottom of the lake a coating of algae, fungi, and bacteria awakes and begins to manufacture oxygen. This gas turns the lake bottom and the tiny organisms living there into a buoyant matting, which rises and becomes embedded in the bottom of the ice cover. The mass continually works its way up through melting ice layers toward the surface. After four or five years, the mat emerges on top as a crinkly, paper-like brown mass with a velvety texture.

The mass then dries and is carried off by the fierce winds of the area, which blow so hard that research huts are often pelted by rocks they pick up. If a segment of this mass lands in tepid water, such as the melting from nearby glaciers, the organisms it contains begin to thrive. Within a few days, they turn the water a blue-green, forming a community of different species of algae, bacteria, and fungi. In this way, life keeps a finger-tip grip on the hostile environment of the dry valley region. Perhaps in an equally remarkable way, life may exist where it is currently believed to be impossible, such as on Mars.

Another of the valley lakes, Don Juan Pond, is quite extensive in area but only two or three inches deep. The big pond is saturated with calcium chloride, a rare combination of molecules that makes the water corrosive. One of the effects of the water is that it dramatically shrinks leather. Visitors are warned not to splash through the pond if they are wearing leather boots. A size ten boot can shrink rapidly to a size six, creating a new form of foot torture. Amazingly, rugged varieties of bacteria manage to live in the pond despite the corrosive nature of the water.

The Sea

Filled with icebergs and floating pack ice, the seas around Antarctica are not only dangerous but are also colder than other oceans. Although the temperature of the water is usually 29° Fahrenheit, no one could live for long in it without some kind of protective suit. Yet antarctic waters team with a profusion of living organisms from tiny krill to giant whales.

Scientists see many interesting aspects of these frigid waters while they study them with the advantages of modern equipment. High-speed winches bring up samples and cores from the ocean floor. An echo-sounder, adapted from sonar equipment, is used to measure the ocean depths continuously and automatically. Echo-sounding measurements give a "picture" of the sea bottom over which a ship has sailed. Seismic sounding, the same method used to measure ice thickness, is employed to reveal the type and thickness of sediments on the ocean floor.

The research ship Hero *off Palmer Station*   U.S. NAVY

Oceanographers from the United States, along with exchange scientists from other countries, work from the research ship *Hero*, a wooden vessel built to augment the facilities at Palmer Station during the summer, as noted. The wood provides resiliency in sea ice and helps keep the ship acoustically quiet. Although diesel powered, the ship has sails to assure steadiness, safety, and the silence which is essential to many of the underwater studies. The *Hero* has four laboratories and a work boat for geological and biological investigations on the Antarctic Peninsula, as well as the oceanographic projects. Ten scientists and a crew of ten comprise the *Hero's* usual complement.

A second research ship, the ARA *Islas Orcadas* (formerly the USNS *Eltanin*) is leased to Argentina and jointly operated by that country's antarctic program and the National Science Foundation. The ship is capable of carrying thirty-eight scientists on sixty-day cruises around antarctic waters. Cameras on board take pictures of the ocean bottom and strange sea creatures. Found only at great depths, these animals had never been seen before they were photographed. They live under great pressure; this and their own internal pressure are such that they explode when hauled up from the deep.

5. Life in a Lifeless Land

PLANTS

Few forms of life can exist in Antarctica because of its cold dry climate and heavy covering of ice. Sunlight is another problem for vegetation, not only because it vanishes for months at a time but also because of its blinding intensity during the summer.

In addition to the harsh climate, few plants can grow in Antarctica because of the lack of soil. But some plants manage to survive on fertilizer left by sea birds nesting on the continent during the summer.

Lichen, a tiny plant composed of alga and fungus, is one of the few primitive plants that grow in Antarctica. Looking like small blotches of color on rocks, these adaptable plants can dehydrate quickly to avoid damage from freezing. Sometimes they return to life after many years. Others seem not to grow at all, as photographs taken over successive seasons indicate.

Although you have to search to find them, lichens grow in many places of the continent. They hold the record for existing in cold weather. Because they can grow on wind-blown manure from coastal bird nests, lichen have been found on mountain peaks within three hundred miles of the South Pole, where it was believed nothing could live. The ability of the stubborn lichen to survive in such tough conditions, in addition to the micro-organ-

isms found in the soil, suggests that life may exist in other places that seem lifeless to us, including other planets.

Scientists have been busy classifying and describing the lichens found in Antarctica. They are eager to know how long these plants have lived there and how they are related to those on other southern continents. It may seem incredible but the relationship of lichens growing on different continents can help explain the history of the world.

Insects

The only native animals of Antarctica are a few tiny insects which can be found in areas free of snow and ice part of the year. The summer sun, beating down twenty-four hours a day, warms the rocks and melts the snow, providing a bit of moisture for the bugs to live on.

A wingless fly about a quarter of an inch long is the largest of these insects. Biologists discovered these flies hopping around pools of melt-water on the Antarctic Peninsula. After careful examination, the scientists determined that the fly of Antarctica was closely related to flies in South America. Such a study and

124

others like it help biologists understand how animals change their appearance over a long period and why they live in different places.

For years biologists suffered cold fingers and toes identifying a grand total of fifty species of insects. Their task wasn't made any easier by such pranks as that played by some Navy helicopter pilots who brought flies in a jar from New Zealand and let them loose in the scientists' quarters. After sending telegrams announcing the startling discovery of flies in Antarctica, the excited scientists were more than a little embarrassed when they were told about the joke.

As a result of the biologists' dedication, we now know that ticks and lice are common but springtails and mites are more widespread throughout Antarctica. Springtails are small, wingless insects that have an appendage which they can extend quickly to "spring" into the air. Mites are like tiny ticks. In Antarctica, they live on plants and on penguins, seals, and birds.

For food, insects that don't live on other animals eat the lichens that grow in the area. Sometimes they eat each other. They can also "turn themselves off" when the weather is especially cold or when they can't find anything to munch on. When conditions improve, they "switch on" and continue about their business.

FLYING BIRDS

Birds adjust most easily to life in Antarctica because they are built to withstand the cold. They have thick, waterproof feathers, thick skins, layers of fat, and practically no exposed skin. In addition, birds are fair-weather visitors to the continent. Like most of the scientists and maintenance personnel, the birds arrive for the summer weather when there is an abundance of food in the sea. When it turns colder, they leave.

But the cold isn't the biggest problem for birds in Antarctica. Life on the Ice is difficult for them because there are so few exposed areas such as rocky cliffs where they can build their nests. Suitable sites often become overcrowded because many different types of birds have to share the same location.

Because of the shortage of coastal sites, some petrels are forced to nest hundreds of miles inland. Small colonies of snow petrels

The south polar skua   T. MASON

and south polar skuas have been found in the mountains 150 miles from the coast. No other animal has been known to live so far south.

Although they are protected from it, the birds lose many of their eggs and chicks each year because of the severe cold. But enough chicks survive to keep the antarctic bird population among the highest in the world.

Scientists are learning more about the habits of antarctic birds through banding programs conducted every year. They catch a few birds and clip metal bands to their legs in order to trace their travels. As a result of this, biologists have found that birds in Antarctica return to the same nests and the same mates each year, despite the hazards they must undergo.

Bird watchers also use satellites to follow the movements of birds, such as the giant petrel that has been tracked all the way around the world. Another remarkable bird, the arctic tern, commutes eleven thousand miles between the Arctic and Antarctica. Whenever the tern finds darkness catching up with it in one place, it takes off and flies to the other end of the world where the sun is shining.

The south polar skua flies great distances, too. From its breeding grounds near penguin rookeries, it wings its way to winter quarters in the floating ice at sea, a distance of over one hundred miles. Sometimes, the skua migrates even further. In 1975, a skua banded on Shortcut Island, near Palmer Station, was found six months later by an Eskimo in Greenland. The skua covered 8700 miles while still very young.

The skua is a gull about the size of a small goose. With its

126

heavy, powerful beak and wings measuring four to five feet, it preys on eggs and the young of other birds. Skuas also eat fish and krill in the sea and garbage around camps.

Skuas have earned the name "eagle of the Antarctic" because of their fierceness in frightening penguins away so they can snatch their eggs. Skuas can also use their sharp beaks to rip open a baby chick's stomach for the food inside. They will even attack a man if he should intrude into their nesting area.

PENGUINS

Although they can't fly, penguins are a type of bird that fascinates everyone. Few birds anywhere in the world can top the feats of the antarctic penguins.

To keep them warm, penguins have thick layers of fat and are almost completely covered with short, stiff feathers that overlap like scales. They have also discovered how to protect themselves from the cold by huddling together.

Penguins hold the trophy for being better adapted to life in the water than any other bird. They are excellent fishermen and swimmers because of their strong wings, which work like flippers, and their streamlined bodies. While swimming, they look like dolphins leaping or "porpoising" through the water. They can swim at a clip of twenty miles per hour and leap up seven feet in the air to get out of the water. Emperor penguins can dive more

Adélies make their home on rock-strewn coastal beaches.   T. MASON

than one hundred feet looking for food under the ice and stay below for twenty minutes at a time.

On snow or ice, however, penguins waddle around awkwardly, using their wings to balance themselves. It's difficult to be graceful when you're trying to walk on slippery ice with short legs and webbed feet. No wonder penguins look a bit comical when they do. But when they're in a rush, they forget about trying to walk and take to tobogganing. They flop down on their bellies and push themselves along with their wings, much as you would oar a boat.

Penguins can also use their strong wings for defense, as some biologists have noted while trying to catch them to put on leg bands. In addition to banding them, biologists have taken penguins to remote spots and tried to lose them. One time they took some penguins in concealed cages to the opposite side of the continent from McMurdo. The penguins found their way back across hundred of miles without any landmarks to guide them. As the result of such projects, biologists have concluded that penguins find their way by using the sun and an inborn sense of what time it is. In other words, they get as much information from the sun as a navigator does by using a compass and a watch.

You might wonder why the penguins bother. Why do they choose to migrate to Antarctica, of all places? If they're kinky for cold, why don't they stay on the pack ice at sea where they spend most of their lives? The answer is that they are safer on the shore of Antarctica when they are raising their chicks. At sea, predators such as leopard seals and killer whales will attack them; on the coast they only have to beware of skua gulls.

Few of the antarctic penguins have been seen outside of the polar region because they have difficulty adjusting to the different environment. They like very cold weather and lots of space to move around. They also catch infection easily, especially a certain kind of fungus disease which kills them in warmer climates.

But during the 1976–77 austral summer, one hundred Adélie and forty emperor penguins were collected in the McMurdo area to be flown to Sea World, Incorporated, at San Diego. First, the penguins were tested to insure they weren't carrying any disease.

The trick to catching a penguin for research is to avoid its strong flippers and sharp beak. U.S. NAVY

Then they were placed in special containers and put on board a plane where the temperature was kept at 23° Fahrenheit. Despite these precautions, about one-third of the penguins didn't survive the journey and the later acclimatization and quarantine at Sea World. More penguins are scheduled to be captured during 1977–78 to replace these.

Long-range plans are to establish a self-sustained breeding colony in a permanent, temperature-controlled environment at Sea World for research and public education. The research will be neurobiology conducted by Dr. Ted Hammel at the nearby Scripps Institute of Oceanography.

The Adélie and emperor are the only two kinds of penguin that establish rookeries on the Antarctic continent, although on occasion other types have been sighted.

Adélies are the shorter of the two species and seemingly are so full of life that a good description of them is "hysterical." They arrive at their breeding grounds in mid-October from as far as one hundred miles at sea. Like most things they do, Adélies turn their arrival into a comical performance. They leap several feet out of the water and come in for a landing feet first. You can't believe your eyes the first time you see an Adélie pop out of the sea, land upright, and shake itself dry as though there were nothing to it.

Sometimes Adélies approach swimming in a large circle. They employ this "Russian roulette" strategy to draw out any leopard seal lurking under the edge of the ice. The leopard seal usuallly has time only to snare one penguin while the others escape. Each penguin takes the chance it won't become the victim.

The male Adélie arrives at the rookery first. He searches through the windswept breeding grounds for his nest from the previous season, or what is left of it after the winter. Rebuilding the nest, the male picks up stones in his beak from gravel scattered around the rookery. Often he steals stones from his neighbors and a battle breaks out when he gets caught. Consequently, the rookeries look and sound like a battle ground during nest-building.

When the female arrives, she has the difficult job of finding her mate among the thousands of birds in the rookery. The male, however, gives her a few hints. He stretches up his head and flaps his wings slowly while calling, "*Gaa, aah, aa!*" Somehow she can distinguish his voice from all the others and makes her way to the nest.

Together, they finish building the nest to keep their two eggs off the frozen ground when the time comes. Sometimes the female arrives and finds that another has taken up residence. While the two females fight it out, the male sits quietly on the nest until one drives off the other.

After a period of courtship that may last two weeks or more, the female lays two eggs in mid-November and then returns to sea, leaving the male to incubate the eggs. The male's first incubation watch usually lasts from seven to ten days, but it may be even longer if the female has far to go to find open sea. Because the male hasn't eaten since he came ashore, he may be starving to death by the time the female returns. She takes over for a similar incubation period while the male fattens up at sea. Thereafter,

Adélie penguin guards its egg on a nest of rocks.

T. MASON

the Adélie parents take turns incubating the eggs until they are hatched.

Peace descends over the rookery during the incubation which takes about thirty-three days. Unless something happens to the eggs, such as an attack by a skua gull, two fuzzy gray chicks hatch almost simultaneously and are fed predigested krill from the crop of whichever parent is there at the time. For the first two or three weeks, the chicks are brooded closely by their parents as they grow rapidly, developing a thicker down.

The parents then leave their chicks in a crèche or large nursery group while they forage at sea. The chicks protect themselves from the cold and the ever-present skuas by constantly changing position. Those on the outside push their way in, forcing those in the middle toward the outside where they will have their turn to face cold and danger. Despite the protection of the crèche, a sudden cold spell or snowstorm can kill hundreds of them.

When the parents return with food, they call out to their chicks in the huddle. Sometimes several hungry chicks come running to be fed. To insure they feed only their own chicks, the parents run around the rookery with the chicks chasing them until all but two give up.

In late December and January, the rookery is visited by "teenagers," young, non-breeding Adélies in their second and third years. Some go through the motions of courtship and nest building, but others act more like teen-age mobs. They beat nestholders and trample on chicks. However, they also may stand in the crèche huddles and help protect the chicks from the skuas. After a few days, they leave for the pack ice at sea.

By late January the chicks are three-quarters grown and begin to molt. With their new juvenal plumage, they wander to the shore and test the water in February. They learn how to swim and, with the adults leading the way, head for the pack ice where they spend the winter feeding on krill and frolicking on the floating ice.

As the Adélies are departing their coastal rookeries, the emperor penguins are beginning to arrive at theirs. In doing so, the emperors must raise their young during the antarctic winter when temperatures are often as low as —60° Fahrenheit. No other animal can survive in such a cold environment.

The emperor penguins, of course, have good reasons for their seeming madness. Because it takes them longer to grow up than the smaller-sized Adélies, emperor chicks are born during the austral winter so that they will mature enough to survive the next winter on their own. The chicks also escape the danger of being eaten by predators. During the winter, the skua gulls, leopard seals, and killer whales all have gone north.

Emperor penguins make their rookeries on the sea ice along the coast of Antarctica, instead of popping ashore as the Adélies do. Their breeding grounds are always located near permanent openings in the ice so they can reach the sea no matter how cold it gets and how thick the ice freezes around them.

The penguins pair off, but they don't build a nest. When one large egg, weighing a pound, is laid in May, the male takes the egg from his partner and, balancing it across his toes, drapes a warm fold of abdominal skin over it. He then settles into a crouching position to begin incubating the egg. Immediately, the

132

Emperor penguins make their rookery on sea ice near open water.

female heads for open water to find food. Both she and her part-ner have starved for the two months during courtship.

But for the male the ordeal is just beginning. While the female is gone, he rocks back and forth on his short, stiff tail feathers to help keep the egg warm. He may also toddle a short distance or toboggan on his belly without dropping the egg from his feet. As it becomes colder, the male joins with thousands of others in sleepy masses where they huddle together very tightly to keep warm. The ones on the outside push their way into the middle when they get cold so that no one constantly must bear the brunt of the freezing winds. By using less energy to produce body heat, the males can exist longer without eating.

During the incubation period, the male emperor survives a fur-ther two-month period without food. By the end of incubation the males are down to nearly half of their original body weight. The female returns as the egg begins to hatch, if all goes well. But sometimes the female can't make it back in time. Should this happen, the male manages to produce small quantities of crop secretion containing fat and protein to feed to the chick.

Relieved at last, the male departs for three to four weeks of feeding at sea. The female takes the chick on her feet and feeds it partly digested food from her crop. The chick grows slowly until

Emperor penguin chick rides on the feet of its parent. U.S. NAVY

the male returns with more food; then the growth rate acceler-
ates. During this period, adults who have lost their chick may join
forces and ruthlessly fight successful parents for their chick.
While the successful parents fight to keep their chick, the little

one is often trodden under foot or killed during the battle.

After seven or eight weeks, the chicks grow a thick gray down and join others in a crèche for mutual protection while the parents race back and forth between the sea and the huddle to bring them food. Many chicks freeze to death despite the crèche if the weather is especially cold or if they haven't been fed well. Other chicks go astray and fall into cracks in the ice.

Those that survive molt their gray down by late December and grow their first-year feathers, a drab gray and yellow version of their parent's glowing plumage. When the sea ice beneath them breaks away from the land, the emperors move with it.

Scientists are unsure whether adult emperors breed every year. Hopefully, the colony at Sea World will provide the answer.

It has been noted that the emperor chick, shown here peering out from under its parent's stomach fold, resembles another "bird," the LC-130 Hercules. U.S. NAVY/T. MASON

SEALS

Seals, particularly the Weddell, are the only animal that can equal the amazing feats of the antarctic penguins in surviving the harsh life in Antarctica. They belong to the same family as the common harbor seal seen in the Northern Hemisphere, although they are slightly different in appearance.

Antarctic seals are called "true" seals, as opposed to fur seals and sea lions. True seals have no external ears and are slightly better streamlined for swimming and diving, but they are more awkward on land. Sea lions and fur seals walk with their bodies off the ground, limbs pulled underneath and flippers sticking out to the side. They can run and easily scramble over rocks. True seals are more like slugs. With shorter fore-flippers and trailing hind limbs, they must slither awkwardly on land by undulating their body muscles. But at sea the combination of tails and hind limbs form a kind of broad propeller that makes them terrific swimmers.

Small herds of Weddell seals are a common sight near coastal stations such as Scott Base. More is known about Weddells than other antarctic seals because their proximity and gentle nature make them easy to study. You can walk up to them and pet them if they aren't with their pups. Weddells have no reason to fear man because in the past they were seldom killed by man. They are now protected by the Antarctic Treaty except for the few that are permitted to be killed to feed the sledge dogs still being used. The population of Weddells is believed to be about four million.

Weddells, which grow up to ten feet long and weigh one thousand pounds, are the slowest, most sluggish seals of all. Nearly half of their weight is blubber. But this heavy insulation of blubber enables them to stay afloat and also gives them a reserve supply of energy on which they can survive if they can't find food in the darkness under the ice.

In addition to their layers of blubber, Weddells keep warm by quickly turning food they have eaten into energy. In fact, antarctic seals can create more energy faster than any land animal of their size. They also have a special heating system which keeps them comfortable in the severest cold. Whenever they want to

Visitor teases Weddell pup. T. MASON

conserve heat, antarctic seals can shrink the blood vessels near the surface of their bodies. This keeps most of their warm blood toward the center of their bodies where it is protected from the cold by the layers of blubber.

This heating system works so well that antarctic seals overheat in warmer waters. For this reason few are ever seen in zoos or aquariums. Those that are in captivity have another problem, particularly Weddells. They must be fitted with tough, platinum-tipped teeth to keep them from ruining their own teeth on the cement walls of their swimming pools, which they apparently mistake for ice that must have a breathing hole in it.

Weddell seals are called the true seals of continental Antarctica because of the amount of time they spend on the ice along the shore. Breeding takes place in the water, and one pup is born on the ice at the beginning of October when the temperature may be as low as −30° Fahrenheit.

The scrawny pup helps to keep itself warm by shivering, which somehow works against the cold, while it grows quickly on its mother's rich milk. In about two weeks, the pup doubles its size and becomes better equipped to endure the cold. At this time the pup enters the water for the first time, although it may be suckled

137

and tended by the mother for another month or more. Parent and pup swim together until it comes time for the pup to emerge from the water. Then the mother often cuts a ramp and helps the pup out of the water with nudges and calls. The males take no part in the pup's rearing, although their presence may be necessary to keep interlopers away and reduce competition for space and food around the breathing holes.

During the winter, the seals live almost entirely in the sea which often freezes up to depths of ten feet. They keep their breathing holes open by gnawing away with their sharp front teeth at any new ice that forms over the holes.

For years biologists have studied the habits of Weddell seals at a place where they congregate a few miles from McMurdo. By lowering underwater television cameras and microphones through the breathing holes, the scientists have been able to observe the seals in the dim light under the ice.

Although mostly silent on land, the Weddells make strange noises underwater that sound like birds chirping in a room full of echoes. Biologists think that the seals use the echoes from their sounds to navigate under water, much as submarines navigate by sending out sound waves that bounce off any object in their path. In this manner the seals locate their breathing holes and find fish in the darkness under the ice. They use other calls, which sound like far-out electronic music to talk with each other, the biologists believe.

Intrigued by Weddell seals, scientists have tracked their movements under water by strapping tiny radio transmitters onto their backs. They discovered that the seals hold the most incredible diving record in the world. They can dive two thousand feet and remain there for as long as forty minutes without coming up for air. While holding their breaths, Weddells can swim, hunt, and eat fish.

Weddell seals also can surface quickly from their great dives without the ill effects caused by nitrogen bubbles forming in the blood and tissues that would injure or kill a human diver. Biologists currently believe that the Weddells accomplish their amazing dives by changing the way the blood circulates in their

138

bodies. This switch enables the seals to hold more oxygen in their blood stream and to withstand the build-up of large amounts of carbon dioxide as well. At the same time, Weddells can turn off any body functions they don't need for swimming.

Sharply contrasted to the gentle-natured Weddell seal is the quick, deadly leopard seal. The fastest seal in the sea, the leopard has a slim body designed to strike and kill quickly. It can leap out of the water and snatch penguins or seal pups from the ice floes.

On land, the leopard can move across the ice as fast as a man jogging, which poses a constant threat to researchers working with seals and penguins. The leopard is also dangerous because it is big. The second largest seal in Antarctica, it grows from ten to twelve feet in length and weighs as much as 850 pounds. A man can't shake off an animal of that size with its teeth embedded in his leg.

As its name suggests, the leopard seal has a large snakelike head and gray-spotted coat. It lives and hunts alone, whereas most other seals group together in herds. The leopard remains in the outer fringes of the pack ice and they come together only at mating time. When no warm-blooded meat is available, it dines on fish and squid. Only one animal, the orca or killer whale, dares to tangle with a leopard seal. A killer whale will attack and kill a leopard seal for food just as savagely as the leopard takes its prey.

Antarctica has other interesting seals, including the strange

Killer whale lurks among the ice floes. U.S. NAVY

Ross seal, which is the smallest member of the family. Few of these dark-colored seals have been seen, but scientists guess that their population is about 50,000. Little is known about them, except that they have high-pitched voices and sound something like humans' singing. For this reason, sailors on the old sailing ships began calling them the "singing seals." Ross seals spend most of their time in the pack ice at sea, probably feeding on fish, squid, and krill.

The biggest seal of all is the huge elephant seal, which breeds on islands near the continent. These brutes weigh up to four tons, of which nearly one third is fat. The bull has inflatable nostrils which hang over the mouth like a trunk and form a resonating chamber. He can produce a trumpeting with this trunk that deafens you if you're close by. The breeding bulls roar and fight continuously while large numbers of cows are forming harems around them on the beaches.

Nearly 97 per cent of all antarctic seals are the beautiful crabeaters which feed on krill, despite their name. About the same size as Weddells, crabeaters have silvery, fawn-colored coats

Elephant seal trumpeting   NATIONAL SCIENCE FOUNDATION

Crabeater seals bask on an ice floe. u.s. navy

when freshly molted in the spring, and they bleach almost pure white in the summer sun. Because they spend all of their time in the pack ice, crabeaters suffer the most of all seals from attacks by killer whales. It's common to see a crabeater seal bearing the triple razor slashes of killer-whale teeth on its sides.

Crabeater seals created one of the mysteries of Antarctica when their carcasses were discovered in the dry-valley region. Other crabeater bodies were found three thousand feet in the mountains. The cold, dry air had preserved them like mummies, adding to the puzzle of how the seals got there and how long they had been there.

Scientists are still arguing the question of how these seals got to the dry valleys. Some believe they became trapped on shore when holes in the ice froze over unexpectedly. With nowhere to go for food, the seals scattered aimlessly. Some wandered inland to the dry valleys and couldn't find their way back to the sea. The often clear trails in the sand picture a long, shuffling trek before death.

Other scientists believe the climate warmed up, which caused the ice to recede southward. The seals moved with the ice, but then the weather changed again, becoming cooler. The ice in-

141

creased northward and the majority of the seals followed it north. Some, however, went the wrong direction and were trapped in the valleys.

Whatever the cause, the mummified seals can still be seen there. By analyzing radio-carbon content in the carcasses, scientists have determined that the seals are from sixteen hundred to two thousand years old. Yet, because they are preserved, some look as if they just came out of the sea.

WHALES

A variety of whales feed on the plentiful antarctic sea life in a zone of about two hundred to three hundred miles around the continent during the spring and summer months. When the sun sets, the whales swim north to warmer waters where they breed and raise their young.

Whales are unique because they are air-breathing mammals of high intelligence that left the land millions of years ago and adapted to life in the sea. Today, whales spend all of their time in the water, except when they surface to take in a large store of oxygen. Their babies are born under water, too, and grow quickly on their mother's rich milk.

Originally four-legged, whales have lost all trace of hind limbs and use their fore limbs as paddles. Their flat tails or flukes drive them forward comfortably at the speed of a slow cargo boat. Although they can travel much faster over short distances, they quickly tire when chased by whalers.

Except for man, whales are the longest living mammal. Most live between seventy-five and one hundred years; the finback lives over one hundred years. During their lives, most of the cows have about twelve babies. Whales therefore would be increasing in numbers because of their long life span if whaling hadn't substantially reduced their numbers.

Whales are also special because of their enormous size. The blue whale, which migrates to antarctic waters, is the largest creature ever to live on earth. This magnificent animal grows from 70 to 100 feet long and weighs 150 tons. Blue whales are bigger even than the great prehistoric dinosaurs.

Both the toothed and the baleen types of whales are found in antarctic seas. The baleen whale filters tons of krill and other plankton out of the sea with a giant "strainer" of whalebone which hangs from the roof of its mouth. You might say this whale swims through the ocean like a huge vacuum cleaner, scooping up the krill.

In addition to the blue whale, five kinds of baleen whales migrate to antarctic waters, including the right, humpback, bowhead, gray, and sei. They average between thirty-five and ninety-five feet in length.

The largest of the toothed whales is the sperm whale, which has twenty-six peglike teeth on either side of its lower jaw but none in the upper jaw. The sperm whale, which was the subject of Herman Melville's classic novel *Moby Dick*, reaches a maximum length of about sixty feet. It is the only toothed whale to match the baleen whales in size. Swimming in pods of fifteen to twenty, the sperm whale usually is found in temperate and tropical waters around the world. Only solitary males, for some unknown reason, wander into polar regions.

The bottlenosed whale, blackfish, dolphin, porpoise, and killer whale are the other members of the toothed-whale family to reach the Antarctic. They feed mostly on squid and fish, although the killer whale also attacks porpoises, seals, penguins, and even larger whales, as noted.

Toothed whales often dive deep in search of their prey, using a variety of sound signals in hunting and communication with each other. They are also highly social. Dolphins and porpoises often form huge schools of several hundred; killer whales hunt in large family groups.

FISH

Antarctica is one of the few places in the world where men sometimes go fishing with sticks of dynamite. The men, however, are scientists, not fishermen, and they dynamite large holes in the ice to reach the fish in the water along the shore. Other scientists spend many months on ships such as the *Hero*.

Three of the sixty-six kinds of fish the biologists have found

A Chaenichthyid, *one of many kinds of fish especially adapted to life in antarctic seas.* NATIONAL SCIENCE FOUNDATION

possess something like antifreeze in their bodies. *Dissostichus mawsoni,* for instance, has the amazing ability to resist freezing because of this substance, even though it lives in water at a temperature of 28.5° Fahrenheit, which would freeze blood and tissue in other animals. Although the scientists know this fish has some sort of protection, they aren't sure as yet how it works, other than to lower the freezing point of the fish's blood. Chemical analysis has revealed that the protective compound consists of salt, amino acids, potassium, calcium, urea, and 50 per cent protein.

When the biologists find out how the antifreeze works in antarctic fish, they hope to learn how an organism can change itself to adapt to life in very cold or hot temperatures. The scientists also hope to copy the antifreeze substance and make an artificial antifreeze which could be used to preserve human blood and tissue for transplanting from one person to another.

They might also learn how to make antifreeze for plants to provide resistance to frost, thereby enabling fruits and vegetables to grow in the winter. The Soviet Union already has begun to try such experiments with frost-resistant plants in Siberia, where crops are limited by the short growing season.

In addition to antifreeze, antarctic fish have other special characteristics, including the ability to change their energy output and grow faster than fish in warm waters. Scientists are eager to learn how they are able to grow faster so the size of fish that live in customary fishing areas can be increased.

6. Natural Resources

HARVESTING SEA LIFE

Because of the biological wealth in the oceans around the continent, Antarctica is attracting attention as an important source of food for the future. Scientists estimate that antarctic seas are four times as productive as other oceans. In summer, some areas of this vast "bouillabaisse" yield more vegetable matter than the best agricultural land. Antarctic waters also produce more carbohydrates, fat, and animal protein than expertly managed pasture land.

The low temperature and high mineral content of the water are responsible for this marine abundance. Because the water is so cold, it can hold much dissolved carbon dioxide and oxygen that plants and animals need for growth. Antarctic seas are also high in nitrogen content because they lack nitrogen-liberating bacteria. In addition, currents constantly churn up minerals from the ocean bottom to the surface where plants can use them for food. The long period of summer sunshine is another boon to the unusual plant growth.

As a result of such conducive conditions, small floating plants called phytoplankton grow by the millions. In some places they tinge the water green or color the ice red-brown or a dark yellow. The minute plankton serve as food for such small floating animals

146

The shrimp-like krill (Euphausia superba) *is a major new source of protein.* U.S. NAVY

as krill. Marine biologists estimate that the antarctic ocean holds 5.6 billion tons of krill. The quantity of krill eaten each year by whales, seals, and birds is three times the amount of fish caught in the world.

Because the plentiful krill are high in protein and vitamin A, seven countries are interested in catching them, particularly the Japanese and Soviets who already have trawlers operating in antarctic waters. Three Japanese fishing companies in 1976 began to advertise krill to drum up public interest. These companies planned to put 7800 tons of krill on the Japanese and international market during the 1976–77 season.

The biggest problem in marketing the krill is that the little crustaceans spoil quickly. Because of a liver enzyme, they turn black in two hours after being netted. Japan and other nations hope to prevent this by fishing from factory ships, which have equipment to freeze the krill or process them into a protein paste. The Soviets have used krill paste since 1970 in cheese and butter products to give them a shrimp taste. Researchers have also processed krill into liquid protein and meal. Such different forms enable krill to be used in many different ways, including as an additive to make food more nutritious.

147

French scientists have found a carotinoid pigment in krill that can be used to make medicine for treating ulcers. Other researchers have discovered that krill can be used on fish farms to enhance the color of salmon and trout so the fish will appear more attractive to eat.

Fishery experts predict one hundred million tons of krill can be caught each year without endangering the species. Conservationists, however, are worried that the removal of large amounts of krill will further threaten the survival of whales, which depend on krill as their main source of food. In addition, there are no laws regulating the catching of krill, which increases the likelihood that fishing companies may take too much and eventually wipe out the krill and the large animals that need them as food.

The eagerness of fishing companies to exploit Antarctica's accessible marine life has lead also to the restoration of sealing. Using the evidence that seals are increasing in numbers, these companies played a major role in convincing the Antarctic Treaty Nations to change the treaty to permit the harvesting of certain species. The treaty convention, ratified by the United States in 1977, enables hunters and scientists to take a specified number of seals in various designated areas each year. Around McMurdo, for example, the quota is fifty Weddell seals. Most of these, as mentioned before, are used to feed the New Zealand dog teams. Some are dissected by scientists before they are given to the huskies so that more efficient use is made out of them.

The convention prohibits any killing of the Ross, elephant, and fur seals because so few of these are left. Unfortunately, there is no way to police this agreement effectively. No Coast Guard exists in Antarctica to catch sealers who break the law. We can only hope that sealers will abide by the treaty agreement and not repeat their historic slaughter of antarctic seals.

Commercial whaling, on the other hand, has continued since 1904 although, due to the lack of conservation measures, the industry has declined until only Japan and the Soviet Union continue to take whales in any substantial number. Other whaling countries, including Australia, Portugal, Peru, Chile, and South Korea, account for less than 10 per cent of the annual catch.

148

Modern whaling ships use radar and sonar, as well as airplanes, to chase down pods of whales. Because of this efficient equipment and the long time it takes for whales to reproduce, some types have nearly become extinct, including the blue, right, humpback, bowhead, and gray.

Quotas on the number of whales that can be caught each year are established by the International Whaling Commission, the IWC, which was set up after World War II to regulate the killing of whales. But the IWC hasn't been effective because not all the countries engaged in whaling belong to it. Moreover, the IWC has no power to enforce the quotas it recommends.

The problem of regulating the industry is complicated by the lack of agreement by scientists on how many whales can be killed each year without endangering the survival of the species. Conservation groups, on the other hand, want all whaling stopped and are trying to pressure Japan and the Soviet Union by boycotting their products.

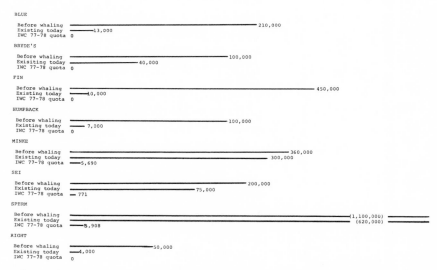

Chart shows the estimated number of whales that scientists believe existed before commercial whaling began in the 19th century, the estimated number of whales existing today, and the numbers of whales that the International Whaling Commission allowed whalers to catch during the 1977–78 season. T. MASON

The United States stopped whaling in 1972, and is among those countries that have tried to save the whales by banning the use of whale products. In these countries whale oil is no longer used for lubricating machinery and making lipstick and margarine, nor are whale bones crushed for fertilizer.

MINERALS

The antarctic environment is also threatened by the likelihood that someone will locate one of the suspected rich mineral deposits and find a way to recover it economically.

Over two hundred minerals have been discovered in Antarctica, although generally not in sufficient quantities to make them of commercial value. The growing shortage of natural gas, oil, and other minerals, however, is forcing nations and corporations to take a second look at geological studies that show areas of Antarctica are similar to mineral-rich spots in the Southern Hemisphere.

Deposits of gold, copper, lead, and tin have been found on the Antarctic Peninsula, which is geologically related to the South American Andes, where vast amounts of these minerals are mined. Eastern Antarctica compares geologically with parts of India, Brazil, Africa, and Australia which have gold, iron, dia-

Coal seam appears as a dark ribbon in exposed sandstone cliffs.

U.S. NAVY

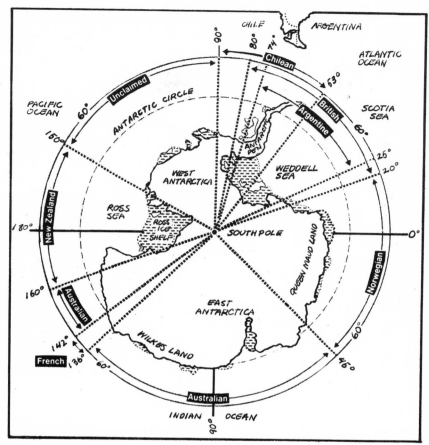

Claims made to antarctic territory   W. CALDWELL

monds, uranium, and coal. Some scientists have said the Transantarctic Mountains would be mined for their coal if the area
wasn't covered with ice and snow.

In the 1976–77 season, new evidence of uranium was gathered
by aerial surveys over areas of the Transantarctic Mountains bor-
dered by the dry valley region west of McMurdo Sound. Using an
airborne instrument to detect gamma rays, researchers from West
Germany and the United States found uranium concentrations
that could have economic importance. Sandstone mountains of
similar age and structure have yielded uranium in India, in the
Karroo area of South Africa, and in the Gabon region of West

Africa where the French find supplies for their nuclear weapons program. The geologists plan to continue their uranium hunt in future years.

Geologists also predict that substantial oil and natural gas fields exist on the Antarctic Peninsula and offshore areas. According to the United States Geological Survey, fifteen billion barrels of oil may be recoverable from offshore regions alone, making Antarctica a major untapped energy source. The improvement of cold-weather technology, such as that used to extract Arctic oil and gas, and the increasing demand for new supplies of oil and natural gas have greatly enhanced the possiblity that oil wells one day will be drilled in Antarctica.

The prospect of mineral exploitation in Antarctica poses a political problem, in addition to a threat to the scientifically important environment. Since all territorial claims are suspended by the Antarctic Treaty, a mining company could set up operations without any nation's permission or control over its activities. In an effort to prevent this, the treaty nations have made a temporary agreement to refrain from commercial exploration until a solution can be found to which everyone can agree.

COLD STORAGE

Antarctica's cold dry climate and vast uninhabited space have prompted speculation that one day the continent could be used to stockpile food surpluses, such as grain and corn, in years of over-productivity. But such a scheme would be economically unfeasible unless huge amounts of surplus food needed to be kept in cold storage, because of the cost of shipping it and keeping it in silos there.

In the past, politicians from several countries have suggested that the continent be used as a dumping ground for waste materials from nuclear reactors. Nuclear-waste disposal is becoming a big problem because more of it is being generated every year. Moreover, there are few places where this deadly material, which remains radioactive for 200,000 years, can be stored safely. A small drop could kill thousands of people over a wide area if the poison leaked from its container. Leaks have occurred in several

Could an ice cave be used for cold storage?   U.S. NAVY

places in the United States but fortunately no people were hurt, although a number of animals died.

So far, the treaty nations have remained firm in their stand against storing nuclear wastes on the continent. They realize that the ice sheet covering the continent is constantly moving. Eventually, the ice would deliver a storage cannister to the sea, if it weren't cracked by the pressure of the ice beforehand, and the poison would come back to us floating on an iceberg.

TOURISM

Of all Antarctica's potential resources, the unique environment probably will continue to be the continent's most profitable resource. Increasing numbers of tourists, eager to say they have been "on the Ice," are being attracted there.

Lindblad Travel of New York City, the principal tour organizer, takes shiploads of camera-toting travelers to Antarctica every year. The tourists are willing to pay between four and ten thousand dollars to spend a few hours on the coast near Palmer or McMurdo stations, mainly because Antarctica is somewhere few people have been.

M.S. Lindblad Explorer sails past melting iceberg on her way to deliver tourists to the Antarctic Peninsula. GEORGE HOLTEN

Companies in Australia and New Zealand have investigated the possibility of building tourist facilities so they can fly tourists to McMurdo, but so far they haven't been able to solve the problems of high cost and safety. Their plans also have been opposed vehemently by scientists who don't want their projects disturbed. As a result, tourist trips by air have been limited to flights over the continent, although a few chartered tourist flights have landed for brief stopovers in the past.

The Sixth Biennial Consultative Meeting of the Antarctic Treaty Nations took the first step to protect Antarctica from tourists in 1971 when they adopted a resolution recommending tours give notice before they arrive. Tourists are also required to follow the instructions of station authorities so that they don't enter reserved areas or disturb research projects.

Despite these regulations, anyone who wishes can go to Antarctica as long as he has the means to get there. But at some point he will need the assistance of a national expedition working on the Ice and be forced to cooperate with them.

PROTECTING THE ENVIRONMENT

In addition to tourists, increasing scientific work and its related support work pose a problem because the plants and animals are highly vulnerable to any kind of disturbance. They are isolated creatures, highly specialized to their barren homeland, which makes them liable to suffer from the slightest outside interference.

Until recently, man considered Antarctica a wasteland so vast and barren that he didn't have to be careful about what he left behind there or the pollution caused by airplanes and ships.

Few studies have been done to indicate the damage man's pollution has done. But there is evidence that penguins and seals have absorbed DDT from McMurdo's waste disposal. The poison, used to kill insects on plants in the United States, was brought to McMurdo in food for the men stationed there. Other nations have been equally guilty of disregarding the antarctic environment.

Fortunately, the situation has changed so that the plant and animal life on the Ice are better protected today than in some

155

Emperor penguins seem to symbolize Antarctica. T. MASON

"civilized" countries. Each nation that claims part of Antarctica has passed regulations to protect the plants and animals in its region. An Adélie nesting on the Antarctic Peninsula, for example, is protected by not one but three sets of laws because Britain, Argentina, and Chile all claim and guard that penguin's rookery.

In addition, the signators of the Antarctic Treaty have agreed to a number of protective measures, including the minimizing of harmful interference with the normal living conditions of the animals, the requirement of a permit to capture or kill any animal, restriction of the importation of animals and plants, and precautions to prevent accidental introduction of parasites and diseases into the region.

At Mawson Station, for instance, the Australians make sure the plants and animals are disturbed as little as possible by the researchers working there. The Australians insure that only the same individual, wearing the same clothes, enters a colony of birds or animals to study them. The colony becomes accustomed to this intrusion and doesn't feel threatened. The Australians also keep their twenty-two sledge dogs tied up so the huskies can't chase the birds and seals.

The New Zealanders send men to the McMurdo area at various times to repair and watch over the historic huts used by the early explorers. They also insure that tourists don't take any of the historic articles left in the huts or approach too close to nearby penguin rookeries.

In addition to cleaning up McMurdo, the United States prohibits its helicopter pilots from flying over penguin rookeries and frightening the birds off their nests.

The protection of Antarctica's most valuable asset, therefore, seems assured for the present. But additional measures, especially one to settle the question of territorial claims, will be needed if the environment is to be safeguarded in the future. At stake is a great reservoir of scientific knowledge and one of the last earth frontiers where you can still find the thrill of adventure in the ultimate earth trip.

Index

Adélie Coast, 61
Adélie penguins, 61, 70, 128, 130–132, 157
Admiralty Range, 62
Air Age, 86–90
Aircraft, 12–22, 27, 31, 37–38, 51, 82–83, 86–94, 97, 104. *See also* Hercules
Alexander I Land, 59
Algae, 119–121, 123
American Highland, 90
Amphibians, 115–116
Amundsen, Roald, 66, 75–76, 78, 81, 89, 91
Amundsen-Scott South Pole Station, 31–32, 39, 49–53, 94
Andes Mountains, 114, 150
Annual sunrise, 43, 86
Annual sunset, 37, 43
Antarctic Development Squadron SIX, 12–26, 33, 37, 45, 51
Antarctic Peninsula, 18, 124, 150, 152, 157
climate of, 55, 106
exploration of, 59–66, 70, 86–87, 91–92
Antarctic Treaty, 22, 30, 96, 136, 154, 157
Arctic, 62, 126, 152
Argentina, 13, 27, 92, 96, 114, 122, 157
Armitage, Albert, 69
Atmospheric research, 51–53, 109–114
Aurora, 84, 86
Auroras, 50, 109–111
Australasian Antarctic Expedition, 82
Australia, 21, 95–96, 103, 109, 157
exploration by, 64, 75, 82, 86, 90
Axel Heiberg Glacier, 78

Bacteria, 119–121
Balleny, John, 62
Barne, Michael, 70
Bay of Whales, 66–67, 76, 78, 87, 90, 93–94
Beardmore Glacier, 72, 79–81, 100
Bellingshausen, Thaddeus, 58–59, 94
Bennett, Floyd, 87
Biology, 75, 119, 123–150
Birds, 123–136. *See also* individual species
Birth, first human, 92
Black, Richard, 91
Blackfish, 143
Blizzards, *see* Snowstorms
Blue whales, 142–143, 149
Borchgrevink, Carsten, 64–65
Bottlenosed whales, 143
Bowers, Henry, 77–82
Bowhead whales, 143, 149
Bransfield, Edward, 58
Bruce, William, 63
Bull, Henrik, 64–65
Byrd, Richard, 53, 87–89, 91–94
Byrd Station, 38, 53, 88, 94, 103–104

Cape Adare, 62, 64
Cape Ann, 60
Cape Bernacchi, 72
Cape Crozier, 66, 68, 70, 77–78
Cape Evans, 76–77, 79, 84, 86, 93
Cape Royds, 72
Car, 71–72
Casey Station, 98

Chapel of the Snows, 45
Cherry-Garrard, Apsley, 77, 82
Chile, 13, 84, 96, 148, 157
Christchurch, N.Z., 12–13, 15–17, 33
Christensen, Lars, 90
Climate, 12, 55, 75, 95, 100–101, 103, 106–109
effect on: buildings, 50; cooking, 31–32, 53, 69; health, 15, 22–24, 30, 32, 53; machines, 22, 51
precipitation, 106–107
use for food storage, 152
storms, *see* Snowstorms
summer, 12, 20, 35, 51
temperature ranges, 106
winds, 16, 107, 109, 115, 121, 133
winter, 15, 37, 77, 132
Clothing, 14, 46, 84, 119
Coal, 70, 80, 151
Communications, 12, 33–35, 77, 112
Continental drift, 118
Cook, Frederick, 66
Cook, James, 56, 58–59
Cooperation, 13, 37–38, 93–96, 105, 109
Cosmic rays, 109, 113–114
Crabeater seals, 140–141
Crevasses, 45, 48, 70, 75, 83
Cruzen, Richard, 92

Darlington, Jenny, 92
David, Edgeworth, 72–73, 75
Davis, John, 60, 64
Deception Island, 59, 86, 114
"Deep Freeze," *see* Operation "Deep Freeze"
Discovery, 66, 68–70
Dissostichus mawsoni, 144
Dogs
used by explorers, 65–72, 75–79, 92
used today, 21–22, 136, 148, 157
Dolphins, 127, 143
Don Juan Pond, 121
Dronning Maud Land, 90–91
Dry valleys, 77, 97, 119–121, 141, 151
Dufek, George, 94
D'Urville, Dumont, 61–62

Earthquakes, 51
East Base, 91–92
Eielson, Carl, 86
Eklund, Carl, 91
Elephant seals, 140, 148
Ellsworth, Lincoln, 89–90
Ellsworth Land, 66, 90
Ellsworth Mountains, 114
Emperor penguins, 70, 127–128, 132–135
Enderby Land, 60, 90–91, 102
Endurance, 84
Environmental protection, 148–149, 152, 155–157
Erebus, 62
Eternity Mountain Range, 90
Exploration, 32, 49, 56–97

Factory ships, 147
Ferrar Glacier, 69–70, 72, 77

Fin whales, 63
Fish, 143–145. *See also* individual species
Flags, 23, 37, 50, 72
Flies, 124–125
Food, 17, 29, 31, 35, 39, 43, 48, 69, 152, 155
Ford Range, 87
Fossils, 115–118
Foyn, Svend, 63
France, 61, 96, 102–103, 105, 148, 152
Fremouw Formation, 118
Frostbite, 22–23, 51–52, 68, 77, 81–82
Fuchs, Vivian, 95
Fungi, 119–121, 123, 128
Fur seals, 58, 90, 136, 148

Garpike, 116
Gates, David, 100
Geology, 72, 80, 114–115, 119–121, 151–152
Geomagnetism, 34, 109–110, 112–114
Gerlache, Adrien de, 66
German expeditions, 71, 75, 91, 151
Glaciers, 17–18, 70, 72, 79–81, 97, 99–100, 114. *See also* individual glaciers
Glossopterid tree, 115
Gray whales, 143, 149

Halley Bay Station, 60
Henson, Matthew, 75
Hercules, 12–22, 27, 31, 37–38, 51, 97, 104
Hero, R/V, 53, 122, 143
Heroic Era, 66, 75–86
Hillary, Edmund, 95
History, 56–97
Hitler, Adolf, 91
Hollick-Kenyon, Herbert, 90
Holmes & Narver, 14, 22, 27, 53
Hughes Bay, 58, 60
Humpback whales, 63, 143, 149
Hut Point, 43, 67–70, 76–78, 82, 86

Icebergs, 58, 62, 101, 121, 154
    formation of, 17, 22, 99–100
    fresh water uses, 101–103
Icebreakers, 13, 18, 20, 24, 30, 60, 92
Ice cap, 50, 104–106, 114
    drilling of, 103–105
    land under, 95–96, 106–107
    melting of, 98–100
Ice cores, 103, 105
Ice shelf, *see* individual ice shelves
Ice studies, 98–106
Insects, 65, 124–125, 155
International Geophysical Year, 50, 93–98
International Whaling Commission, 149
Ionosphere, 34, 109, 112
Islas Orcadas, ARA, 122
Isolation, 26, 30, 33–35, 37–38, 40–44. *See also* Wintering over

Japan, 58, 75, 96, 114–115, 147–149
Jensen, Bernhard, 65

Kaninan Bay, 94
Killer whales, 76, 128, 132, 139, 141, 143
King Edward VII Land, 67, 71
King George V Land, 82
Knox Coast, 93–94
Krill, 121, 127, 131–132, 140, 143, 147–148
Kristensen, Leonard, 64
Kukri Hills, 77

Labyrinthodont, 115–116
Lake Bonney, 120

Lakes, 77, 93, 97–105, 116, 119–121
Lake Vanda, 120
Larsen, Carl, 63
Larsen Ice Shelf, 65, 101
Lashley, William, 70
Leopard seals, 128, 132, 139
Lice, 125
Lichen, 123–125
Lindblad Travel Company, 55, 154
Little America camps, 87–88, 93–95
Lystrosaurus, 116–118

Mackay, Dr. Alistair, 72–73
Mackintosh, Aeneas, 86
McMurdo Sound, 20, 24, 29–30, 155
    exploration of, 63, 68–69, 72, 76–77
McMurdo Station, 12, 20–21, 27–49
    construction of, 93–94
    facilities, 28–30, 33–35, 43
Macquarie Island, 82
Mac-Robertson Coast, 89
Magnetic field, *see* Geomagnetism
Magnetic pole, *see* individual poles
Mapping, 56, 81, 88, 90–93
Marie Byrd Land, 53, 88, 94
Mawson, Douglas, 72–73, 75, 82–83, 95
Mawson Station, 157
Meteorites, 103, 114–115
Meteorology, *see* Climate
Micro-organisms, 103, 119–121, 123–124
Mid-winter's day, 43
Mikkelsen, Caroline, 91
Minerals, 102, 150–152
Minnows, 116
Mirny Station, 94
Mites, 125
Morning, 69
Motor sledges, 21, 75–76, 78
Mountains, 114. *See also* individual mountains
Mount Erebus, 20, 24, 62, 141

National Aeronautics and Space Administration, 101
National Antarctic Expedition, 66
National Science Foundation, 11, 14, 27, 30, 51, 53, 105, 122
New Zealand, 21–22, 39, 45, 56, 64–66, 90, 96
    protection of historic sites, 157
    relations with U.S., 12–14, 97

Oates, Captain Lawrence, 79–82
Observation Hill, 43, 82
Oceanography, 43, 82
Odd I, 102
Oil, 150–152
Operation "Deep Freeze," 11, 14, 27, 93–94, 97
Operation "High Jump," 92–93

Pack ice, 57–58, 62–63, 84, 121, 132, 139–141
Palmer, Nathaniel, 58–60
Palmer Station, 27, 53, 55, 122, 126, 154
Peary, Robert, 66, 75
Penguins, 61, 70–71, 125, 127–128, 130–135, 155, 157. *See also* individual species
Personnel, 11, 14, 26–27, 40, 132–135
Petrels, 125–126
Plankton, 146
Plants, 55, 64, 70, 114–115, 123–125, 145–146, 155, 157. *See also* individual species
Polar plateau, 49, 52, 69–70, 72, 78, 93, 107
Pollution, 29–30, 51, 109, 155

Ponies, 43, 71–72, 75, 78–79
Ponting, Herbert, 75–77
Porpoises, 143
Possession Island, 62
Post office, 33–34. *See also* Communications
Princess Astrid Coast, 104
Princess Martha Coast, 101
Princess Ragnhild Coast, 89

Queen Mary Land, 82
Queen Maud Land, 58, 60, 104

Radio operations, *see* Communications
Reptiles, 115–117
Resolution, 115–117
Right whales, 63, 143, 149
Riiser-Larson, Hjalmar, 89
Ritscher, Dr. Alfred, 91
Robertson Bay, 64–65
Roberval, Canada, 112
Rockefeller Mountains, 87
Rocks, 65, 70, 78, 81, 103, 114–115, 123
Ronne, Edith, 92
Ronne, Finn, 91–93
Ronne Ice Shelf, 72
Ross, James, 61–64
Ross Ice Shelf, 22, 24, 62, 66, 70, 100
   drilling of, 104–105
   exploration of, 62, 67, 72
Ross Island, 12, 20–21, 23, 29, 45
Ross Sea, 18, 62, 64, 66, 83, 86, 88, 95, 105
Ross seal, 60, 63, 140, 148
Royal Geographical Society, 66
Royal Society Range, 62
Royds, Charles, 68

Saudi Arabia, 102
Scotland, 60, 63, 75
Scott, Robert, 21, 43–44, 66–72, 75–82, 84, 93, 95, 97
Scott Base, 14, 21–22, 24, 39, 43, 45, 49, 136
Scurvy, 69, 86
Sealing, 58, 60, 62, 64, 148
Sea lions, 136
Seals, 24, 136–142. *See also* individual species
Sea World, 128, 135
Sei whales, 143
Sentinel Mountain Range, 90
Shackleton, Ernest, 66–69, 71–72, 75, 79, 83–84, 86, 95, 115
Shipping, 12–13, 18, 20, 27, 30, 53, 55, 91
Shortcut Island, 126
Siple, Dr. Paul, 53
Siple Station, 53, 112
Skiing trip, 45–49
Skua gulls, 125–126, 128, 131, 132
Snow blindness, 68, 80
Snow melters, 30
Snowstorms, 62–63, 107
   effect on flying, 16–17, 38
   danger to surface travel, 25–26, 45, 68, 72, 78–79, 81–82, 84, 86
Solar storms, 15, 34, 95
Sometimes, The, 33
Southern Cross, 65–66
South Georgia Island, 58, 84
South Geographic Pole, 21, 39, 49, 52–53, 123
   climate of, 51–52, 106, 110
   role in exploration, 63, 66, 69–72, 75–83, 87, 91, 93, 95, 97
   research at, 50–52
South Magnetic Pole, 62, 64, 71–72, 75
South Pole Station, *see* Amundsen-Scott South Pole Station

South Sandwich Islands, 58
South Shetland Islands, 58, 84
Soviet Union, 37–38, 93, 95–96, 105, 147–149
   explorers, 58–60, 94, 102
   research by, 94–95, 100, 104–105, 145
Space program, 119
Sperm whales, 63, 143
Springtails, 125
Stonington Island, 91
Stress, *see* Isolation
Swedish expedition, 70
Syowa Base, 58, 115

Taylor, Griffith, 77–78, 97, 119
Taylor Glacier, 70
Taylor Valley, 77
Temperatures, *see* Climate
Tern, Arctic, 126
Terra Nova, 76–77, 82
Territorial claims, 22, 95–96, 152, 157
Terror, 62
Ticks, 125
Tourists, 51, 55, 154–155, 157
Tracked vehicles, 16, 21, 72, 88, 105. *See also* Weasel
Transantarctic Mountains, 18, 20, 24, 62, 69–70

United Kingdom, 13, 21, 114, 157
   exploration by, 58, 60–86, 90, 92, 95–96
   research by, 104–105
United States, 13–14, 33–34, 150
   concern for environment, 29–30, 148, 155
   exploration by, 58–61, 75, 86–97
   research, 97, 102–105, 122, 151–152
United States Antarctic Service Expedition, 91
United States Geological Survey, 152
United States Navy Antarctic Task Force, 11–12, 14, 22–27, 30, 33, 40, 125

Victoria Land, 17, 62, 66, 69, 72–73, 77
Vince, George, 68
Vinson Massif, 90
Volcanoes, 20, 24, 62, 71, 114
Vostok, 59
Vostok Station, 93–94, 96, 106
VXE-6, *see* Antarctic Development Squadron SIX

Washing, 29–30, 35, 84, 97
Waste disposal, 29–30, 127, 152–155
Weasel, 45, 48–49
Weddell, James, 60
Weddell Sea, 60, 63, 71, 83–84, 86, 88, 95, 101
Weddell seals, 21, 30, 60, 136–140, 148
West Germany, 96, 151
Whales, 142–143. *See also* individual species
Whaling, 63, 84, 90–91, 94, 102, 142, 148–149
Whistlers, 112
Whiteout, 25–26
Wilhelm II Coast, 71
Wilkes, Charles, 60–62
Wilkes Land, 93
Wilkins, Hubert, 86–87
Williams Field, 16, 20, 22–24
Wilson, Dr. Edward, 68, 70, 77–82
Winds, *see* Climate
Wintering over. *See also* Isolation
   conditions during, 15, 28, 36–39, 51
   by explorers, 65, 68–69, 71, 77, 84–86, 88
Women, 91–92, 96–97
World War II, 91, 149
Worst Journey in the World, The, 77